Quick & Easy
Dump
Dinners ™
and More

By Cathy Mitchell

Telebrands Press
79 Two Bridges Road
Fairfield, NJ 07004

www.telebrands.com

ISBN: 978-0-9895865-6-6

Manufactured in USA
15 14 13 12

About Cathy:

Cathy has been cooking for 60 years, starting at her Grandmother's side, standing on a stool. She never refers to herself as a chef, but rather a great home cook who enjoys making simple, easy meals with ordinary ingredients. She has been sharing those ideas on television since her first commercial in 1989, introducing America to the electric sandwich maker, and in typical
Cathy fashion, making a lot more than sandwiches. Her kitchen has always been the gathering place for friends and family and she loves to share her recipes and cooking hints while she prepares meals or snacks, often testing out new recipes on a willing group of "Tasters". She has an extended family of 5 adult children, ranging in age from 31 to 43, and 10 grandkids from 1 to 20. One of her favorite stories is overhearing her oldest son's response, when a dinner guest commented before dinner that he didn't really like something on the menu.
He said, "Well maybe not before, but you haven't tried my Mom's yet!"

TELEBrands PRESS

TABLE
of Contents

Introduction to Dump Cooking

If you're like most people trying to lead a busy life in the modern world, you probably often rely on things like fast food and pizza delivery for dinner. You know eating this way is unhealthy and expensive, yet you can't seem to find the time to get a healthy, home-cooked meal on the table for your family. Many people have simply given up on the idea of cooking because it seems so time consuming and stressful, so you're not alone.

You probably think that the type of person that cooks home cooked meals for their family everyday has a gourmet kitchen, loads of fancy high end cooking appliances, and tons of time to spend in the kitchen slaving away. Not to mention that fresh ingredients are expensive and difficult to prep if you don't have expert kitchen skills. Who has the time, money, and resources to learn how to cook from scratch?

What if I told you that you can cook dinner every night, eat a delicious, healthy dinner with your family, and not have the added stress of expensive ingredients, endless chopping and prepping, and a sink full of dishes when you're done? Impossible, you say? Not hardly.

Dump cooking is a technique that allows you to simply "dump" a variety of ingredients into a pot, pan, or casserole dish, turn on the heat or pop it in the oven, and turn out delicious, healthy meals that the whole family will love. In most cases, you only use one cooking vessel along with a few utensils, so dishes and clean up is practically non-existent. With minimal effort, you'll whip up meals that are super easy, super fast, and most importantly, absolutely delicious.

In this book, you'll find recipes for practically any type of dish you can think of. Soups, appetizers, casseroles, and even breakfast can be prepared with minimal effort. You'll learn how to prepare certain ingredients that will be staples in your meals so that you always have them on hand when you don't know what to make for dinner. For even less effort, there are also plenty of meals you can prepare that contain five ingredients or less. Yes, you can prepare a delicious meal with only a few ingredients, and I'll show you how.

What's the Catch? Do I Have to Have a Huge Kitchen or Expensive Cooking Equipment?

Here's the beauty of dump cooking: Anyone can do it. If you have an oven and stovetop, you can cook these delicious meals. You don't need top of the line cookware, and you don't need special tools that look like they belong in a professional kitchen. If you have basic pots, pans, and utensils, you are all set to put amazingly delicious meals on the table in no time flat. You don't need a big kitchen; room on your counter top will do.

Do I Need to Spend Hours in the Kitchen? I Work All Day and I'm Hungry When I Get Home.

Hours in the kitchen? Who has time for that? The whole purpose of these recipes is so that you can come in the door, spend a few minutes putting together your dish, and then get it started on the stove. While it's cooking, you can relax after a long day, or catch up with the kids. Then, it's time to sit down and eat.

What About Ingredients? Do I Need Fancy, Expensive Ingredients From a Special Store?

Relax. Everything you need for the recipes in this book can be found in your normal grocery store. Most of the items usually go on sale at some point. With proper planning, these meals can easily be made to fit within any budget. You won't have to source ingredients from an expensive gourmet market; you won't have to wander down the aisles looking for an ingredient you've never heard of or can't pronounce. These recipes are made from foods you know and love.

The beauty of these meals is that they are easy for anyone, yes *anyone,* to prepare. You don't need special skills, special cookware, or a ton of time. All you need is the desire to feed your family healthy, delicious meals quickly and efficiently. If you've got that, you're ready for a whole new outlook on cooking!

How to Make Dump Cooking Even Easier

Dump cooking is as easy as it gets, but there are a few things you can do to make it easier. Follow these tips and tricks to get the most out cooking for your family.

- Do as much as you can ahead of time. Instead of spending precious time in the kitchen on a Tuesday night after a long day, try setting aside a few hours on a Sunday afternoon to prep for the whole week. The recipes in the Make Ahead section of this book will help you get started.
- Instead of measuring out herbs and spices, try seasoning blends or packets. Taco seasoning can be used for more than tacos, and a packet of ranch seasoning can be added to everything from dips to soups to casseroles to add flavor quickly without dirtying up a set of measuring spoons.
- Make a meal plan for the week. It doesn't take long, and then if you know what you're making for dinner, you can get all the ingredients out of your cupboard in the morning before you head to work. When you get home after a long day, all you have to do is throw everything in the pot/pan/dish, cook and you're ready to sit down and eat!

- Have leftover stock or sauce? Freeze it in ice cube trays and then store the cubes in a freezer bag. Two cubes is about 1/4 a cup, so you don't need to get any measuring cups or spoons dirty; simply throw the right amount of cubes in your pot and you're good to go!
- Many meals, such as casseroles and soups, freeze extremely well. Make double batches of your favorites and store them in the freezer to reheat later. This way, when you're not up to cooking, you can take out a freezer meal instead of heading to a fast food joint.
- Keep a stocked pantry. Frozen and canned veggies, dried pasta, and canned beans are all staples that can be turned into meals in minutes. Have a few cans of chicken stock ready to go.
- Invest in tools that will help you do things faster. A food processor will quickly shred chicken, grate cheese, or dice veggies. An immersion blender allows you to puree soup directly in the pot so you don't have to go the hassle of transferring to a blender and blending in batches. You don't need everything, but look out for the tools and equipment will make your family's favorite meals easier to prepare.
- Speaking of tools, an ovenproof skillet is a solid investment. This allows you to start your meal on the stove and finish in the oven without having to transfer the contents to a casserole or baking dish. This means fewer dishes.
- One of my favorite kitchen tools is the **Pasta Boat Microwave Pasta Cooker**. It's unbeatable for cooking rice or pasta for your meal without having to use a separate pot or pan. It also takes the guesswork out of cooking these staples. It comes with a cookbook to cook different types of pasta, but to cook rice, simply put 1 cup of long grain rice and 2 1/4 cups water in the Pasta Boat. Microwave UNCOVERED for 15 minutes for perfect rice every time.
- Remember, just because a recipe calls for canned corn, that doesn't mean you can't use frozen if that's all you have. The best way to save money is to use what you have on hand. Leftovers make great soups, which are also a great way to use up veggies that are near the end of their lifespan. Leftovers can also be used in creative new ways. Meatloaf can be turned into square meatballs; pot roast makes great stews and soups. Don't be afraid to use your imagination and come up with your own recipes.

Products I Love That You'll Love Too!

Here are some products and seasonings that I use in my everyday cooking. I've given some suggestions, but feel free to experiment based on your tastes. That's half the fun of cooking after all!

- **Morton's Nature Season:** This blend of salt, pepper, garlic, onion, and celery seed is great on anything you want to add just a little flavor to. Try it on veggies, as a quick rub for meats, or whatever else you can think of

- **Lawry's Seasoned Salt:** This is a favorite in my house. Perfect for meat, chicken, fish, and as an addition to marinades or gravy.

- **Mrs. Dash Table Blend:** This is just a good all around seasoning that's perfect when you just don't know what you're looking for. For the best baked or fried chicken you've ever had, use a mix of this and Lawry's; you'll never look back!

- **Better than Bouillon:** This comes in a little jar and is in paste form. It comes in beef, chicken, and veggie flavors and tastes better than canned stocks.

- **Kitchen Bouquet:** This little bottle is like magic! It works great to brown up chicken or beef, and it gives gravy or other sauces richer flavor.

- **Knorr Pasta and Rice Sides:** Sometimes you just need a quick and easy side dish, and these fit the bill. A variety of flavors make these a go to side or light meal in our house.

- **Idahoan Instant Mashed Potatoes:** Everyone loves mashed potatoes, but who has time to make them from scratch? Until I discovered Idahoan, I always made mine. My favorite is the Baby Reds, but try them all until you find your favorite and you'll be surprised at how often you make mashed potatoes!

- **Lipton Onion Soup Mix:** This adds savory flavor to all kinds of things from hamburgers to meatloaf to roasts. I buy several packets at a time and store them in a jar and just use a tablespoon or two where it seems fitting.

Short Cuts and Substitutions

The recipes in this book are created with one goal in mind: making a quick dinner that tastes delicious and doesn't require a lot of cleanup.

With that in mind, everyone is different, but we all want to save money and eat a little better right? In this section, you'll find some more ways to make getting dinner on the table a little easier, while saving money at the same time.

Short Cuts to Save Time

These are easy time savers that will help you get your cooking done quicker and easier with a little prep work. When you look at my recipes throughout the book, ingredients that can benefit from these will be marked in parentheses, so (TS1) means you can save time by using the first one.

Time Saver No. 1

When you come home from the store with ground beef, buy 4 or 5 pounds and then put it in a large deep pan, cover with water and cook over a medium heat, stirring occasionally until meat has no pink color. Drain in a large colander, divide, and then transfer to plastic storage bags or containers. You can freeze or refrigerate until ready to use.

Hint: If you cooked 5 pounds divide into 5 bags so you have 1 pound servings = to recipe calling for 1 pound ground beef, cooked and drained. If you store in a large container, 2 loosely packed cups = about 1 pound. 6 pounds cooked will = 4 bags of 1 1/2 pounds for recipe calling for 1 1/2 pounds cooked and drained ground beef, or about 3 loosely packed cups. This will work for all dump recipes calling for ground beef and eliminate the extra step of stovetop browning. If there is water in your recipe, use 90% lean ground beef and you won't have to precook!

Extra tip: Another way to save time is to use 90% lean ground beef if your recipe calls for water. There's no need to precook that way, and because there's less fat, there's no draining!

Time Saver No. 2

When on sale, buy boneless, skinless chicken breasts. Put in a large deep pan, cover with water and simmer until chicken has no pink inside (about 30 to 45 minutes). Remove from water, allow to cool, then shred or cube, and pack in plastic bags. I use one sandwich bag for each breast piece cooked. 1 bag = 1cup shredded or chopped, cooked chicken.

Time Saver No. 3

Instead of taking the time to chop onions every time you need them, do it ahead of time. If you have to chop one onion, why not chop several? I find it much easier to get everything out once in the week than every night. You can store chopped onions in a airtight container in the fridge for up to a week. This also works for bell peppers, celery, and carrots.

Time Saver No. 4

Whether you make your own broth or buy canned, you can freeze in ice cube trays. Once it's frozen, transfer to freezer bags. Two cubes equals about 1/4 cup.

Time Saver No. 5

If you have a favorite packaged seasoning blend (mine is Lipton Onion Soup), buy several at a time and store them in a mason jar or other sealed container. This way, you can control the amount of seasoning you use. One envelope is equal to about 4 tablespoons.

Time Saver No. 6

Have a recipe that calls for bacon bits or cooked bacon? Cook up extra bacon with your Sunday breakfast and crumble it. Store in an airtight container in the fridge for up to a week. You can also buy pre cooked bacon bits in the same aisle as the salad dressing (Hormel is a favorite of mine.)

Time Saver No. 7

Want to always have bacon on hand? I keep a package in my freezer at all times. When I see a recipe that calls for a slice or 2 of raw bacon, I stand it on its side. I then use a bread knife and slice through all of the slices. A 1/2 inch slice equals about two slices of bacon, and the best part is that you don't have to thaw or chop it, since it crumbles as it cooks!

Time Saver No. 8

Use the **Pasta Boat Microwave Pasta Cooker** to cook pasta and rice instead of dirtying up another pan. You can cook any type of pasta in it, but you can also cook rice that comes out perfectly every time with 1 cup rice and 2 1/4 cups water. Cook for 15 minutes, and you've got your side covered!

Substitutions That Will Save You Money

We all want to save money in the kitchen, and these are easy ways to do it. When you're looking at my recipes, those that can benefit will be marked with parenthesis, so (MS1) means the first one applies, and so on.

Money Saver No. 1

Want to make your own taco seasoning? Combine 1/2 cup chili powder, 1/4 cup onion powder, 1/8 cup ground cumin, 1 tablespoon garlic powder, 1 tablespoon paprika and 1 tablespoon salt in a jar and shake to combine. One packet of store bought taco seasoning is about 4 tablespoons.

Money Saver No. 2

Canned or homemade stock is nice, but it goes bad quickly and takes up room. Instead buy bullion cubes. You can add them to a pot or pan along with the appropriate amount of water and they don't go bad. Want to increase the chicken flavor in your dish? Add an extra cube.

Money Saver No. 3

Make your own Lipton Onion Soup Mix. Combine 2/3 cup dried minced onion, 1 tablespoon dried parsley, 2 teaspoons onion powder, 1 teaspoon celery salt, 1 teaspoon salt, 1 teaspoon sugar and 1/2 teaspoon pepper in a jar and shake to combine. One packet equals about 4 tablespoons.

Money Saver No. 4

Have a recipe that calls for heavy cream? Substitute canned evaporated milk in equal parts. It makes soups and sauces extra creamy, and you don't have to worry about it going bad. Keep a few cans in your pantry for such an occasion. It's also less expensive.

Money Saver No. 5

Want to make your own gravy mix? Take a jar of chicken or beef instant bouillon (equal to 1/2 a cup) and mix with 1 1/2 cups flour and a teaspoon pepper. One packet of instant gravy mix is approximately 3 tablespoons.

Money Saver No. 6

Love adding Ranch flavoring to your favorite meatloaf or dips? Make your own with this easy recipe. Combine 5 tablespoons dried minced onions, 2 tablespoons parsley flakes, 1 tablespoon salt and 1 teaspoon garlic powder. One packet equals about 2 tablespoons.

Money Saver No. 7

You may not always have buttermilk on hand, but chances are you have milk in the fridge. In a pinch, you can make your own buttermilk with one cup of milk and one tablespoon white vinegar or lemon juice.

Money Saver No. 8

Make your own Italian dressing seasoning by combining 3 tablespoons Italian seasoning, 1 tablespoon garlic powder, 1 tablespoons onion powder, 1 teaspoon pepper, and 1 tablespoon salt in a jar. Shake to combine. Makes the equivalent of one packet of dry Italian dressing mix.

Money Saver No. 9

Make your own fajita seasoning by combining 2 teaspoons chili powder, 2 teaspoons cumin, 1/2 teaspoon garlic powder, 1/2 teaspoon dried oregano, and 1/4 teaspoon salt. Makes 1 packet of seasoning.

Make Ahead Recipes to Make Cooking Easier

While the recipes in this book were created to making cooking delicious meals as easy as can be, this section proves that that can be done even *easier*.

These simple recipes are to be made as part of your meal. Once cooked, you can store your ingredients in the fridge or freezer to make busy weeknight cooking a breeze. You'll also find recipes for many of the seasonings in the Cost Cutters, Shortcuts, and Substitutions sections laid out and easy to follow.

One thing to remember when using these recipes is that you want to make sure all cooked foods are cooled completely before sealing and storing. Not doing so can not only steam your food, making it mushy, but it can lower the temperature of your refrigerator or freezer, and you may even run the risk of food born illness.

Chicken Breasts

Ingredients:

Boneless, skinless chicken breasts (1 medium sized breast makes about 1 cup chopped or shredded chicken
Water

Directions:

1. Bring a large pot of water to a boil. Add the chicken breasts and reduce to a low simmer. Simmer until the chicken is cooked through, 10-15 minutes depending on the size of the breast.
2. Once cooked, allow to cool and either chop or shred. Store in airtight containers in the fridge for a week or in the freezer for up to 3 months. If you're going to freeze, freeze in 1 cup portions so that you can take out what you need for your recipe.

Tip: If you have a stand mixer, use the paddle attachment to quickly and painlessly shred multiple breasts at a time.

Extra tip: In recipes calling for cooked chicken, you can almost always start with raw if that's what you have. Simply slice it up and cook it in a little oil in your pan before adding any of the other ingredients. This is especially true for casseroles and other dishes that are going in the oven anyway. Just make sure your chicken is cooked through before serving, and you should be fine.

Whole Chicken

Ingredients:

1 3-4 pound chicken
1 tablespoon vegetable oil

Directions:

1. Preheat oven to 425 degrees F.
2. Brush the chicken with the melted butter and then place it in an oven proof skillet, with the breasts up.
3. Roast for 15 minutes. Turn the oven down to 375 and continue roasting for about 50 minutes. Test the doneness of the chicken by inserting a meat thermometer in the inner thigh; it should read 160.
4. Remove from the oven and allow to cool before pulling the meat from the bones. Store the meat in small portions in the fridge for up to a week, or the freezer for up to 3 months.

Tip: If you're going to be using the chicken meat to add to recipes, don't be tempted to salt it before cooking. Your recipes will have enough salt on their own, so salting your meat runs the risk of your final meal being too salty.

Ground Beef

Ingredients:

Ground beef (I rarely buy less than 4-5 pounds)
Water

Directions:

1. Put the ground beef in a large deep skillet. Cover with water and cook until no longer pink.
2. Drain, cool, and divide by the number of pounds. Store in Ziploc bags or airtight containers (2 cups equals 1 pound)
3. If you know you're going to use it in a few days, refrigerate it. If not, freeze until needed. This is a great time saver!

Tip: If your recipe calls for water, you can use 90% lean ground beef and avoid having to pre-cook or drain the meat. Just add your beef and your water at the beginning of the recipe and then continue on.

Rice

Ingredients:

2 cups white rice
4 cups water

Directions:

1. Bring the water to a boil on the stove. Add the rice and reduce heat to low. Cover and set a time for 20 minutes. Turn the heat off and leave covered for 5 minutes.
2. Remove lid, fluff with a fork and store in 1 cup portions in the refrigerator for up to a week or freezer for up to 3 months.

Tip: You can make as much or as little rice as you want. Simply double the amount of liquid as raw rice. Remember that rice doubles in volume after its cooked, so 1 cup raw rice will become 2 cups cooked. Since rice goes with just about any meal or dish, you can always find a way to use leftovers if you have it.

Extra Tip: If you don't already have a Microwave Pasta Boat, it makes cooking rice as easy as cooking pasta. Take 1 cup of long grain rice and 2 1/4 cups water and microwave UNCOVERED for 15 minutes for perfect rice guaranteed!

Pasta

Ingredients:

1. 1 pound dried pasta of your choice
2. 4 quarts water
3. 1 tablespoon vegetable oil

Directions:

Bring water to a boil. Add pasta and cook until done according to the package directions. Drain, toss with the oil, and allow to cool.
When cool, store in plastic freezer bags in 1-2 cup portions. Store in the fridge for a week. When needed, you can either reheat the pasta for 1 minute in a pot of boiling water or toss the pasta in a skillet dish to reheat.

Tip: For those times when you don't have cooked pasta on hand and you just don't want to wash any more pots, get yourself a Microwave Pasta Boat. It cooks all types of pasta perfectly, it's dishwasher safe, and easy to clean!

Perfectly Cooked No Splatter Bacon

Ingredients:

1 pound bacon

Directions:

1. Line a sheet pan with foil and lay the bacon slices on the pan so that they don't touch.
2. Put the pan in a COLD oven and turn it on to 400. Set a time for 15 minutes.
3. When the timer goes off, check the bacon. It should be golden brown, but not super crispy, as it will continue cooking when it comes out of the oven. This may take as few as 15 minutes, but could take as long as 20 depending on the thickness of your bacon.
4. Remove from oven and allow to cool completely. Crumble and store in an airtight container in the fridge for several weeks. When using, 1 tablespoon crumbled bacon is equal to 1 slice.

Beans

Ingredients:

1 pound dried beans of your choice

Directions:

1. Soak the beans overnight by covering with about 10 cups water.
2. When ready to cook, drain and rinse.
3. Put in a pot and cover with 10 cups water. Bring to a boil and reduce to a simmer.
4. Simmer for 60-90 minutes, depending on the size of the beans. When they can be easily mashed with a fork, they are done. Drain and cool.
5. Store in airtight containers in the refrigerator for 4-5 days or the freezer for up to 3 months. One 14 ounce can of beans is about 2 cups, so store your beans in 2 cup portions for easier use.

Veggies

Ingredients:

4 cups diced vegetables (broccoli, carrots, potatoes, peppers, onions or whatever you have)
2 tablespoons vegetable oil

Directions:

1. Preheat oven to 400 degrees F.
2. Toss the vegetables with the oil and lay on a sheet pan in a single layer.
3. Roast for 30-45 minutes, until veggies are tender. Allow to cool, and store in container in the fridge. I like to have these on hand for omelets, casseroles, or an easy heat and eat side dish that's healthy and delicious when I don't have time for much else.

"Trashcan" Stock

Named because you use items you would otherwise throw in a trashcan, this quick and easy vegetable stock is perfect for adding extra flavor to pasta water, rice, or soups.

Ingredients:

1 gallon size freezer bag of veggie trimmings (onion skins and pieces, celery leaves and trimmings, carrot and other root veggie skins except potatoes, mushroom trimmings, leek or green onion trimmings; virtually anything you have will work)
6 quarts water

Directions:

1. Add the trimmings and water to a large pot and bring to a boil.
2. Reduce heat and simmer for 45 minutes. Turn off heat and allow to cool.
3. Freeze in ice cube trays for easy use. Once frozen, transfer cubes to a freezer bag or sealed container. Two cubes are equal to 1/4 cup. Sometimes I'll just add a cube to my pasta water to give it just a bit more flavor than plain water.

Tip: I keep a gallon size freezer bag in my freezer specifically for this. Whenever I have trimmings, I add it to the bag and pop it back in the freezer. When the bag is full, it's time to make the stock, but I don't have to do it right then. Sometimes, I'll have more than one bag ready. This assures I don't waste anything!

Perfect Hardboiled Eggs

Ingredients:

6 eggs (more or less, depending on how many you'll go through in a few days)

Directions:

1. Put the eggs in a saucepan large enough that they will fit in a single layer.
2. Cover with at least an inch of COLD water. Bring to a boil.
3. Cover and turn off the heat. Set a timer for 10 minutes. Carefully drain the eggs and cool.
4. Store in an airtight container in the fridge for 5 days. Use for additions to vegetable salads, egg or potato salads, or even as a quick snack!

Tip: Want easy to peel eggs? Let them sit in the fridge for a week before cooking them. If you've already cooked fresh eggs, let them sit in the fridge for a couple days before eating.

Homemade Lipton Onion Soup Mix

Ingredients:

2/3 cup dried minced onion
1 tablespoon dried parsley
2 teaspoons onion powder
1 teaspoon celery salt
1 teaspoon salt
1 teaspoon sugar
1/2 teaspoon pepper

Directions:

1. Put all ingredients in a jar and shake. Store at room temperature. Four tablespoons mix equals one packet.

Ranch Seasoning

Ingredients:

5 tablespoons dried minced onions
2 tablespoons parsley flakes
1 tablespoon salt
1 teaspoon garlic powder

Directions:

1. Put all ingredients in a jar and shake. Store at room temperature. Four tablespoons mix equals one packet.

Italian Dressing Seasoning

Ingredients:

3 tablespoons Italian seasoning
1 tablespoon garlic powder
1 tablespoons onion powder
1 teaspoon pepper
1 tablespoon salt

Directions:

1. Put all ingredients in a jar and shake. Store at room temperature. Four tablespoons mix equals one packet.

Taco Seasoning

Ingredients:

1/2 cup chili powder
1/4 cup onion powder
1/8 cup ground cumin
1 tablespoon garlic powder
1 tablespoon paprika
1 tablespoon salt

Directions:

1. Put all ingredients in a jar and shake. Store at room temperature. Four tablespoons mix equals one packet.

5 or Less: Quick, Delicious Recipes in No Time

Whether you just don't feel like going to the store, or you just want to use up what you have in your pantry, sometimes, cooking with fewer ingredients is a must.

Does this mean you want to have boring meals? Of course not! Which is why these recipes are some that I rely on for just those reasons. I want to eat delicious food, and please my family, but I am strapped for time/ingredients/energy. Whatever the reason, you'll appreciate having these recipes on hand; I know I do!

Deeply D'Lish Pizza
Serves 4

Ingredients:

1 tube Grands biscuits
1 cup marinara sauce (I use Prego)
Pepperoni slices (I used Hormel Turkey Pepperoni)
Sliced olives
1 cup mozzarella cheese shredded

Directions:

1. Cut each biscuit into 6 pieces and drop in bottom of glass or ceramic baking pan sprayed with nonstick spray.
2. Cut pepperoni slices into quarters and distribute over biscuits.
3. Add sliced olives and then a light layer of sauce, about 1 cup. (Add in blops, and do not cover entire surface)
4. Sprinkle with light layer of cheese.
5. Bake at 350 25 to 30 minutes.

Tip: You can use any toppings as long as they will cook properly in 25 minutes. Avoid raw meat.

Easy Smothered Pork Chops
Serves 4

Ingredients:

4 regular cut bone-in pork chops
1 can cream of mushroom soup
1 cup uncooked rice, (not instant)
One 16 ounce bag frozen peas
1 envelope Lipton Onion Soup Mix

Directions:

1. Preheat oven to 375 degrees F.
2. Spray 9 x 13 pan with nonstick spray.
3. Dump mushroom soup, rice, and 2 cups hot water into pan and stir together until well mixed.
4. Stir in peas.
5. Place pork chops on top, pressing down into rice mixture.
6. Sprinkle envelope of dry soup mix evenly over all.
7. Bake 1 hour until chops are done and rice has absorbed liquid.

Spaghetti Carbonara
Serves 6

Ingredients:

4 slices bacon, diced
1 pound hot cooked spaghetti
2 eggs, beaten
1 cup grated Parmesan cheese

Directions:

1. Heat a large skillet over medium heat. Add the bacon and cook until crisp.
2. Turn off the heat and add the cooked pasta and stir in the eggs and cheese.
3. Stir until well combined and heated through before serving.

BBQ Pork Chops with Stewed Apples
Serves 4

Ingredients:

1 tablespoon butter
4 boneless pork chops
1/2 cup barbecue sauce
2 apples, cored, peeled, and sliced

Directions:

1. Preheat oven to 350 degrees F.
2. Heat a large oven proof skillet over medium high heat. Add the butter and pork chops, cook until chops are browned on both sides. Add the barbecue sauce and apples around the pork.
3. Bake for 10-15 minutes, until apples are done and pork is tender.

Baked Honey Dijon Chicken and Potatoes

Serves 4

Ingredients:

1 pound red potatoes, quartered
1 cup honey mustard salad dressing
1 tablespoon chopped onion
8 chicken thighs

Directions:

1. Preheat oven to 400 degrees F. Spray a baking sheet with cooking spray.
2. Toss all ingredients in a large bowl or plastic bag. Lay in an even layer on the baking sheet.
3. Bake for 45-50 minutes, until chicken is cooked through and potatoes are tender.

Best Ever Chicken Parmesan
Serves 4

Ingredients:

4 boneless, skinless chicken breasts
1/2 cup Italian style bread crumbs
1/2 cup grated Parmesan cheese
2 cups marinara sauce, warmed
Hot cooked pasta, for serving

Directions:

1. Preheat oven to 350 degrees F. Lightly spray a baking sheet with cooking spray.
2. Moisten the chicken breasts with water. Combine the bread crumbs and cheese and put in a plastic bag. Add the chicken and shake until all breasts are evenly coated.
3. Lay on the sheet pan and bake for 25-30 minutes, until chicken is cooked through.
4. Serve with the marinara and hot pasta.

Chicken Nacho Casserole
Serves 6

Ingredients:

2 cups chopped or shredded cooked chicken (TS2)
3 cups tortilla chips
2 cups shredded cheddar or Mexican style cheese
1/2 cup sour cream
1/4 cup chopped green onions

Directions:

1. Preheat oven to 350 degrees F. Layer the chicken, nachos, and cheese in a 9x13 casserole dish.
2. Bake for 10 minutes, until cheese is melted. Remove from oven and allow to cool slightly.
3. Top with sour cream and green onions prior to serving.

Beef and Broccoli Stir Fry
Serves 6

Ingredients:

1 tablespoon vegetable oil
1 pound sirloin steak, sliced
1 bag frozen broccoli florets
1/2 cup prepared Asian sesame salad dressing
Hot cooked rice, for serving

Directions:

1. Heat a large skillet over medium high heat. Add the oil and the steak and cook for 1 minute. Add the broccoli and the salad dressing and continue cooking until broccoli is crisp tender.
2. Serve over rice.

Tex Mex Skillet

Serves 6

Ingredients:

1 pound ground beef
1 16-ounce jar corn and black bean salsa
1 cup uncooked white rice
1 cup shredded cheddar cheese

Directions:

1. Heat a large skillet over medium heat. Add the beef and cook until no longer pink in the center. Add the salsa, rice, and 1 cup water. Cover and cook for 20 minutes, until rice is tender.
2. Uncover, turn off heat and add the cheese. Serve when cheese is melted.

Easiest Chicken Quesadillas
Serves 4

Ingredients:

2 cups chopped or shredded cooked chicken (TS2)
1 16-ounce jar salsa
1 cup shredded cheddar cheese
8 flour tortillas

Directions:

1. Preheat oven to 350 degrees F.
2. Combine the chicken and salsa in a large bowl and stir until chicken is well coated.
3. Lay half the tortillas on a sheet pan. Divide the chicken mixture over the tortillas. Sprinkle with cheese. Top with remaining tortillas.
4. Bake for 10 minutes, until cheese is melted and tops of tortillas are lightly browned and crisp.

Italian Stir Fried Chicken and Veggies
Serves 4-6

Ingredients:

1/4 cup Italian dressing
2 boneless, skinless chicken breasts, cubed
1 bag frozen Italian style vegetables
1/4 cup grated Parmesan cheese
Hot cooked pasta or rice, for serving

Directions:

1. Heat a large skillet over medium heat. Add the dressing and the chicken and cook until chicken is browned on all sides.
2. Add the vegetables and continue cooking until tender. Stir in the cheese.
3. Serve with the pasta or rice.

Chicken and White Bean Soup
Serves 4

Ingredients:

2 cups chopped chicken breasts
3 cups chicken stock (TS4)
2 cans white beans, drained
1 tablespoon Italian dressing seasoning
1 10-ounce package frozen spinach, chopped

Directions:

1. Combine all ingredients in a large saucepan with 2 cups water. Bring to a boil and reduce to a simmer.
2. Simmer for 10-15 minutes, until chicken is cooked through and soup is hot.

Southwest Stuffed Baked Potatoes
Serves 2

Ingredients:

2 large Russet potatoes
1 cup cooked black beans
1 cup corn kernels
1 cup prepared salsa

Directions:

1. Preheat oven to 400 degrees F. Prick the potatoes with a fork and wrap in foil. Put in the oven and bake for 45-60 minutes until they pierce easily with a fork.
2. Combine the black beans, corn, and salsa in a saucepan and heat over medium heat until heated.
3. When potatoes are cooked, slice them open and top with filling.

Tip: If you're looking for a change, try enjoying the filling inside some sweet potatoes instead. You can bake them the same way. In our house, I make a big batch of the filling and bake each person's choice of potato for a light, yet filling meal.

Southwest Chicken Soup
Serves 6

Ingredients:

2 cups chopped or shredded cooked chicken (TS2)
2 cans Rotel tomatoes, undrained
1 can corn, undrained
1 can black beans, undrained
1 tablespoon taco seasoning (MS1)

Directions:

1. Combine all of the ingredients in a large pot with 4 cups water.
2. Bring to a boil, reduce to a simmer and simmer for 10 minutes, or until heated through.

Roasted Chicken and Sweet Potatoes
Serves 4

Ingredients:

1 tablespoon vegetable oil
2 sweet potatoes, peeled and cubed
1 onion, cut into wedges
1/2 packet Ranch dressing seasoning (MS6)
8 chicken thighs

Directions:

1. Preheat oven to 400 degrees F. Spray a baking sheet with cooking spray.
2. Toss all ingredients in a large bowl or plastic bag. Lay in an even layer on the baking sheet.
3. Bake for 45-50 minutes, until chicken is cooked through and sweet potatoes are tender.

Broccoli, Bacon, and Parmesan Penne
Serves 4

Ingredients:

4 slices bacon, cooked and crumbled (TS6)
1 bag frozen broccoli florets
1/2 cup grated Parmesan
1 can evaporated milk
1/2 pound penne pasta, cooked according to package directions

Directions:

1. Combine bacon, broccoli, cheese, and milk in a medium saucepan and bring to a simmer. When broccoli is heated through, add the pasta and stir.

Corn and Sausage Chowder

Serves 4

Ingredients:

1 tablespoon vegetable oil
3 Italian sausage links, sliced
1/2 packet ranch dressing seasoning (MS6)
2 cans creamed corn
1 can evaporated milk

Directions:

1. In a medium saucepan, heat the vegetable oil. Add the sausage links and cook until browned.
2. Add the ranch seasoning, stir and add the creamed corn and evaporated milk. Stir and cook until heated through.

Creamed Italian Chicken Pasta
Serves 4

Ingredients:

1 tablespoon vegetable oil
3 boneless, skinless chicken breasts, cubed
1 packet Italian dressing seasoning
2 cans evaporated milk
1/2 pound fettuccine noodles, cooked

Directions:

1. Het a large skillet over medium heat. Add the oil and the chicken and cook until browned. Add the seasoning packet and stir. Add the evaporated milk and bring to a simmer.
2. When heated through, stir in the pasta and simmer until heated through.

Meatball Casserole
Serves 6

Ingredients:

1 bag frozen meatballs
1/2 pound pasta, such as penne or rigatoni, cooked according to package directions
3 cups marinara sauce
2 cups shredded mozzarella cheese

Directions:

1. Preheat oven to 350 degrees F. Spray a 9x13 casserole dish with cooking spray.
2. Layer the meatballs, pasta, and marinara sauce with half of the cheese.
3. Cover and bake for 45 minutes, until meatballs are heated through.
4. Uncover, top with remaining cheese and bake for 10 more minutes, or until cheese is browned and bubbly.

Tip: In our house, this must be served with garlic bread. Simply pop a frozen loaf in the oven when you put the casserole in for the second time, and you'll have a complete meal for no more work!

Creamy Chicken Tortellini Bake
Serves 4

Ingredients:

1 16-ounce bag frozen cheese tortellini
2 cups chopped or shredded cooked chicken (TS2)
1 32-jar Alfredo sauce
1 cup shredded mozzarella cheese

Directions:

1. Preheat oven to 350 degrees F. Spray a 9x13 casserole dish with cooking spray.
2. Combine the tortellini, chicken and Alfredo sauce in the dish. Cover with foil and bake for 30 minutes.
3. Uncover and top with the cheese. Continue baking for 10-15 minutes until cheese is browned and bubbly.

Orange Chicken Stir Fry
Serves 4

Ingredients:

1/2 cup orange juice
2 tablespoons soy sauce
3 boneless skinless chicken breasts, sliced
1 bag frozen mixed vegetables of your choice (a mix of onions and peppers is my favorite, but use your favorite)
Hot cooked rice, for serving

Directions:

1. Heat a large skillet over medium high heat. Add the orange juice and soy sauce and the chicken and cook for 1 minute. Add the vegetables and continue cooking until chicken is cooked through and veggies are crisp tender.
2. Serve over rice.

Roasted Apricot Chicken and Cauliflower

Serves 4

Ingredients:

3 boneless, skinless chicken breasts, cubed
1 bag frozen cauliflower florets
1 tablespoon vegetable oil
1/4 cup apricot jam
Hot cooked rice, for serving

Directions:

1. Preheat oven to 400 degrees F. Spray a baking sheet with cooking spray.
2. Combine the chicken, cauliflower, vegetable oil, and jam in a freezer bag. Shake until well coated.
3. Lay on prepared baking sheet in a single layer and roast 30-35 minutes, until chicken is cooked through and cauliflower is tender.
4. Serve with the hot rice.

Quick and Easy Casseroles

Everyone loves a good casserole. They're enough to feed a crowd, and they're usually hearty and filling. With the recipes in this section, you'll be amazed at just how easy it is to put together a quick casserole, pop it in the oven, and have a delicious hot meal ready in no time.

In this section, you'll find recipes for dishes you didn't think could be so easy. One of the best things about a casserole is that you can get it ready and forget about it until you're ready to eat. They also make great dishes to take to parties and potlucks. A good casserole is also delicious for leftovers. If I've got a busy week ahead of me, you can bet you'll see a few casseroles on the menu!

Best Baked Ravioli

Serves 4 to 6

Ingredients:

1 bag (25 Oz. Bag) Frozen Ravioli, your choice of meat,
cheese, or veggie
1 jar (26 Oz. Jar) Marinara Sauce
2 cups Shredded Mozzarella Cheese
2 cups fresh baby spinach
Parmesan Cheese

Directions:

1. Preheat oven to 400°F.
2. Spray bottom and sides of a 9x13 rectangular baking dish with cooking spray.
3. Spread 3/4 cup of the pasta sauce in baking dish. Arrange half of the frozen ravioli in a single layer over the sauce; top with half of the remaining pasta sauce and half of the mozzarella cheese.
4. Spread spinach over cheese and repeat layer, starting with ravioli, remainder of sauce, and rest of cheese. Sprinkle with Parmesan cheese.
5. Cover with aluminum foil and bake for 30 minutes. Remove foil; bake uncovered for 10 to 15 minutes longer or until bubbly and hot in the center. Let stand for 10 minutes before serving.

Tater-Tot Casserole
Serves 4

Ingredients:

1 pound browned, ground beef
1/2 envelope Lipton onion soup mix
(about 1 heaping tablespoon)
1 (10 1/2 ounce) can condensed cream of celery
or cream of chicken soup (undiluted)
1 16 ounce package frozen tater tots
1 cup shredded cheddar cheese

Directions:

1. Preheat oven to 375 degrees.
2. In a casserole dish, combine cooked ground beef & dry onion soup mix, and cream soup.
3. Top mixture with tater tots.
4. Bake, uncovered, for 30-40 minutes till bubbly and tots are golden brown.
5. Remove from oven & top with cheese, return to oven until melted.

Garlic Bread and Meatball Casserole
Serves 6-8

Ingredients:

6 slices bread
1 tablespoon olive oil
1 teaspoon garlic powder
1 32-ounce jar marinara sauce
1 1-pound bag frozen meatballs
2 cups shredded mozzarella cheese

Directions:

1. Preheat oven to 350 degrees F. Spray a 9x13 casserole dish with cooking spray.
2. Lay the bread in the casserole dish. Top with the meatballs and pour the sauce overtop. Don't drown the meatballs in the sauce; you want your garlic bread o be slightly crispy around the edges.
3. Top with the cheese. Bake the casserole for 30 minutes, until meatballs are heated through and bread is lightly toasted.

Beef and Bean Enchilada Casserole

Serves 4-6

Ingredients:

1 pound cooked ground beef
1 Tablespoon dried minced onion
One 15-ounce can pinto beans, drained
(I use Bush seasoned recipe beans)
One 4-ounce can diced green chilies
1 cup sour cream, mixed with 2 tablespoons flour and
1/4 teaspoon garlic powder
Eight 6-inch corn tortillas
1 1/2 cups enchilada sauce
1 1/2 to 2 cups mixed Cheddar- Jack cheese

Directions:

1. Preheat the oven to 350 degrees F. Spray a 2-quart baking dish with nonstick spray.
2. Mix meat, onion, beans and chilies together
3. Place half of the tortillas in the bottom of the prepared dish, tearing them apart as needed to cover the bottom (overlapping
4. is fine). Top with half of the meat mixture, spoon half of the sour cream mixture on top of the meat, and drizzle 3/4 cup of the enchilada sauce on top of that. Repeat the layers one more time.
5. Cover with foil and bake for 40 minutes. Uncover, sprinkle with cheese and bake an additional 5 minutes or until the cheese bubbly and melted.

Chili Mac
Serves 6-8

Short name...Long on Flavor!

Ingredients:

1 pound lean ground beef
3 cups hot water
1 can (15 ounce) tomato sauce
1 envelope chili seasoning (I use Chili-O by French's)
1 box, 16 ounces, rotini or elbow macaroni
Velveeta slices

Directions:

1. In a large deep skillet or Dutch oven with a cover, place ground beef, tomato sauce, chili seasoning and water. Bring to a boil, stirring a little to break up the hamburger.
2. Once water is boiling, add uncooked pasta, stir, cover and reduce heat. Let simmer about 15 minutes, until water is absorbed by pasta, stirring to mix.
3. Remove from heat, completely cover top with sliced Velveeta, then cover and allow to stand until cheese is well melted.

Note: This has been a family favorite for over 40 years. According to everyone who has ever eaten this, it MUST be served with buttered corn kernels. Never add the corn to the recipe...I tried once and nobody would eat it!
So...put a 1 pound bag of frozen corn in a covered pan with 1/3 cup water, salt and pepper and 2 tablespoons butter.
Cover and cook about 10 minutes, just until water is gone and only the butter is left. Do not drain. At my house the spoonful of corn must go on top of the mac! Nobody spoiled at my house!

Chili Dog Casserole
Serves 4-6

Ingredients:
2 cans (15 ounce each) chili with beans
8 hot dogs
8 flour tortillas (6 inch)
1/2 cup Shredded Mild Cheddar Cheese

Directions:

1. Heat oven to 400ºF.
2. Spread chili into bottom of 11 x 7 inch baking dish.
3. Place 1 hot dog on each tortilla; roll up. Place, seam-sides down, over chili.
4. Spray lightly with nonstick spray to aid in browning tortilla.
5. Bake 15 min. or until hot dogs are heated through and tortilla is browned.
6. Sprinkle with cheese and bake until cheese is melted, about 5 more minutes.

Doritos Cheesy Chicken
Serves 4-6

Ingredients:

2 cups precooked chicken, chopped or 2 cans chicken breast (like Swanson's) drained.
1 cup sour cream
1 can cream of chicken soup
1 can Rotel tomatoes or 1 1/2 cups chunky salsa
1 can corn, drained
2 cups shredded cheese, like Colby Jack or Mexican, divided
1 bag Nacho Cheese Doritos, coarsely crushed or any
leftover tortilla chips (4 to 5 cups or more)

Directions:

1. Preheat oven to 350 degrees F.
2. Spray 9 x 13 pan with nonstick spray
3. Cover bottom of pan with 1/2 of the crushed chips (I often use plain chips here and save Doritos for the top)
4. Dump all other ingredients in a bowl, saving half the cheese.
5. Mix together and pour over chips
6. Top with remaining chips and bake for 20 to 25 minutes until hot
7. Sprinkle remaining cheese over the top and return to oven until melted

Tip: I serve with 1 package prepared Spanish rice, Like Knorr Fiesta Sides
My family likes to fill warm flour tortillas with the chicken!

Buffalo Chicken Casserole
Serves 6

Ingredients:

3 cups shredded cooked chicken (TS2)
2 tablespoons Tabasco sauce
1/2 1-lb. box penne or rotini pasta, cooked
1 can condensed cream of celery soup
1/4 cup blue cheese dressing
1 cup shredded cheese

Directions:

1. Preheat oven to 350 degrees. Spray a casserole dish with cooking spray.
2. Combine everything except for half of the shredded cheese in a large bowl.
3. Pour mixture into casserole dish. Top with leftover cheese.
4. Bake for 25 minutes until casserole is hot and bubbly.

Gumbo Casserole
Serves 6

Ingredients:

2 cans condensed cream of chicken soup
1 cup water
1 teaspoon onion powder
1/2 teaspoon Cajun seasoning
1/2 teaspoon garlic powder
1 cup frozen okra
3/4 cup instant white rice, uncooked
1 1/2 cups diced, cooked ham
1/2 pound peeled and deveined cocktail shrimp

Directions:

1. Preheat oven to 350 degrees. Combine all ingredients in a 2-casserole dish.
2. Bake for 30-35 minutes, until rice is tender.

Chicken Taco Bake
Serves 6

Ingredients:

4 cups shredded or chopped cooked chicken (TS2)
2 cans condensed cream of chicken soup
1 cup sour cream
1 can Rotel tomatoes, undrained
1 can black beans, rinsed and drained
1 package taco seasoning (MS1)
4 cups crushed tortilla chips
2 cups shredded Mexican or cheddar cheese

Directions:

1. Preheat oven to 350 degrees F. Spray a large casserole dish with cooking spray.
2. Combine the chicken, soups, sour cream, Rotel tomatoes, black beans and seasonings in a bowl and stir.
3. Spread half of the chicken mixture in the casserole dish. Sprinkle with half the tortilla chips and cheese. Repeat.
4. Bake for 20-25 minutes until cheese is bubbly.

Beefy Tater Tot Bake
Serves 4

Ingredients:

1 pound ground beef (TS1)
1/2 cup chopped onion (TS3)
1 can condensed cream of mushroom soup
1 tablespoon ketchup
1/2 package frozen tater tots (about 2-3 cups)

Directions:

1. Preheat oven to 400 degrees F.
2. Heat a medium skillet over medium heat and add the ground beef and he onion. Cook until it is no longer pink in the center. Drain
3. Add the soup and ketchup and stir until well combined and pour mixture in a 2 quart casserole dish. Top with tater tots.
4. Bake for 25-30 minutes, until tater tots are golden brown in color.

Turkey and Noodles
Serves 8

Ingredients:

2 cans condensed cream of mushroom soup
1 cup milk
2 cups frozen peas
2 cups shredded or chopped cooked turkey (TS2)
4 cups egg noodles, cooked
2 tablespoons bread crumbs
1 tablespoon melted butter

Directions:

1. Preheat oven to 350 degrees F.
2. Combine the mushroom soup, milk, peas, turkey, and noodles in a 3 quart casserole dish.
3. Sprinkle with the breadcrumbs and drizzle with the melted butter.
4. Bake for 30-35 minutes until top is browned, and casserole is hot and bubbly.

Hot and Spicy Sausage Bake
Serves 6

Ingredients:

1 pound hot Italian sausage
1 cup chopped onion (TS3)
1 cup chopped green bell pepper
1 cup chopped celery
1 cup uncooked white rice
2 cans cream of mushroom soup
1 cup milk

Directions:

1. Preheat oven to 350 degrees F.
2. Heat a medium skillet over high heat. Add the sausage and cook until browned.
3. Add the chopped vegetables, soup, rice and milk. Fill one of the soup cans with water and add that as well.
4. Pour the mixture into a 3 quart casserole dish and bake for about 45 minutes, until hot and bubbly.

Cheesy Cornbread Casserole
Serves 6-8

Ingredients:

1 can condensed cream of mushroom soup
1/2 cup milk
2 large eggs
1 can corn kernels, drained
1 jalapeño pepper, minced
1 8-ounce package cornbread mix (I like Jiffy)
1/2 cup grated cheddar cheese
1 can French fried onions

Directions:

1. Preheat oven to 350 degrees F.
2. Combine the soup, milk and eggs in a 2-quart casserole dish. Mix well.
3. Add the corn, jalapeño pepper, corn muffin mix, and half of the French fried onions.
4. Bake for 30 minutes. Remove from the oven and top with the leftover onions and cheddar cheese.
5. Bake for 10 more minutes until hot and bubbly, and onions are brown and crispy.

Cheesy Chicken and Potatoes
Serves 6

Ingredients:

1 package frozen hash brown potatoes
4 cups chopped raw chicken (TS2)
1 can condensed cream of potato soup
1 8-ounce container sour cream
1 package shredded cheddar cheese (about 2 cups)
1/2 cup milk
1 package Lipton onion soup mix (MS3)
1/2 cup cooked and crumbled bacon (TS6)

Directions:

1. Preheat oven to 350 degrees F. Spray a 13x9 casserole dish with cooking spray.
2. Spread the potatoes evenly on the bottom of the dish. Cover with the chicken.
3. Combine the soup, sour cream, half the cheese, milk, and onion soup in a medium bowl. Pour this mixture over the chicken and potatoes.
4. Cover and bake for 40 minutes. Remove from oven and top with the leftover cheese and the bacon.
5. Bake for 10 more minutes until cheese is bubbly.

Holiday Casserole
Serves 6

Ingredients:

1 can condensed cream of chicken soup
1 cup water
1 can frozen green beans
3 cups chopped or shredded cooked chicken or turkey (TS2)
1 6-ounce box seasoned stuffing mix (I like StoveTop)
1/2 cup grated Parmesan cheese

Directions:

1. Preheat oven to 350 degrees F. Lightly grease a 2 quart baking dish with cooking spray.
2. Combine the soup, water, green beans, chicken, and stuffing mix in a large bowl.
3. Spread into greased dish and baking for 20 minutes. Top with the cheese.
4. Bake for 10 more minutes until top is browned and casserole is bubbly.

Meat Loaf Casserole
Serves 4-6

Ingredients:

1 pound cooked ground beef (TS1)
2 cans condensed cream of mushroom soup
1 packet Lipton onion soup (MS3)
2 soup cans water
2 tablespoons butter
1/2 cup milk
2 cups instant mashed potatoes

Directions:

1. Preheat oven to 350 degrees F. Lightly grease a 2 quart baking dish with cooking spray.
2. Combine the cooked beef with the mushroom soup, onion soup, and 1 can water.
3. Heat the other cup of water, milk, butter, and potatoes in a medium saucepan. Cook until thickened.
4. Spread the beef mixture in a casserole dish and top with the potatoes.
5. Bake for 30 minutes, until potatoes are browned.

Creamy Southwest Chicken Pie
Serves 6-8

Ingredients:

1 16-ounce jar picante sauce
1 can condensed cream of chicken soup
1 8-ounce container sour cream
1 cup shredded cheese
1 can corn kernels, drained
2 cups chopped or shredded cooked chicken (TS2)
1 can black or pinto beans, drained
1 package prepared piecrusts (Package should contain 2 crusts)

Directions:

1. Preheat oven to 400 degrees F.
2. Combine the picante sauce, chicken soup, sour cream, cheese, corn, cooked chicken, and beans in a large bowl. Spread in a 3 quart baking dish.
3. Lay the piecrusts side by side on top of the casserole dish so that the whole dish is covered. Trim excess and press the crusts to seal. Using a pairing knife, cut the pie crust in several spots to vent.
4. Bake for 40 minutes, until crust is browned.

Louisiana Sausage and Rice
Serves 6-8

Ingredients:

1 pound bulk hot sausage
1 small can sliced mushrooms
1 cup chopped celery
1 cup chopped bell pepper
1 cup chopped onion (TS3)
1 6-ounce package seasoned wild rice mix
2 cups chicken stock (TS4)
1 can condensed cream of chicken soup
1 cup shredded cheese

Directions:

1. Preheat oven to 350 degrees F.
2. Heat a medium skillet over medium high heat and add the sausage. Cook until browned and drain off any fat.
3. Add the vegetables, and seasoning packet from the rice and stir. Add the rice, stock, and chicken soup.
4. Pour mixture into a 3 quart baking dish and bake for 1 hour. Remove from oven and top with shredded cheese.
5. Bake for 10 more minutes, until cheese is melted and bubbly.

Tip: If you have an ovenproof skillet, you can bake this dish right in it and skip the casserole dish. This means fewer dishes to wash; who doesn't love that?

Italian Chicken and Pasta Casserole
Serves 6

Ingredients:

1 can condensed cream of chicken soup
1/2 cup water
1 packet Italian dressing mix (MS8)
1 10-ounce package frozen spinach, thawed and drained
2 cups chopped or shredded cooked chicken (TS2)
2 cups cooked penne pasta
1/2 cup grated Parmesan cheese

Directions:

1. Preheat oven to 350 degrees F.
2. Combine all ingredients except the cheese in a medium bowl. Spread in a 3 quart casserole dish.
3. Bake for 30 minutes. Remove from oven and top with cheese.
4. Bake for 10 more minutes until top is browned.

Cheesy Chicken and Noodles
Serves 6

Ingredients:

1 can condensed cheddar cheese soup
1/2 cup milk
1 cup frozen peas
2 cups chopped or shredded cooked chicken (TS2)
4 cups cooked egg noodles
1/2 cup shredded cheese

Directions:

1. Preheat oven to 375 degrees F.
2. Combine the soup, milk, peas, chicken, and noodles in a large bowl.
3. Transfer to a 2 quart casserole dish.
4. Top with cheese and bake for 20-25 minutes until top is bubbly and browned.

Hot Chicken Salad

Serves 8

Ingredients:

2 cups chopped or shredded cooked chicken (TS2)
1 cup cooked rice
3 hard boiled eggs, chopped
2 tablespoons chopped onions (TS3)
1 tablespoon chopped celery
1 can condensed cream of chicken soup
1 cup mayonnaise
1 cup shredded cheese

Directions:

1. Preheat oven to 350 degrees F.
2. Combine chicken, rice, eggs and vegetables in a large bowl. Add the soup and mayo. Spread the mixture evenly in a 3 quart casserole dish.
3. Bake for 45 minutes. Remove from oven and top with the cheese.
4. Bake for 10 minutes until cheese is melted and bubbly.

Sloppy Joe Bake
Serves 5

Ingredients:

1 pound ground beef (TS1)
1 can condensed tomato soup
1/4 cup water
1 teaspoon Worcestershire sauce
1 tube refrigerated biscuits

Directions:

1. Preheat oven to 350 degrees F.
2. Combine the cooked beef with the soup, water, and Worcestershire sauce.
3. Transfer mixture to a 2 quart casserole dish. Top evenly with the biscuits.
4. Bake for 15-20 minutes, until biscuits are browned.

Chicken and Veggie Pasta
Serves 8

Ingredients:

1 can condensed cream of chicken soup
1/2 cup water
1 bag frozen mixed vegetables of your choice (I like broccoli, cauliflower, and carrots)
2 cups chopped or shredded cooked chicken (TS2)
4 cups cooked bow tie pasta
2 tablespoons seasoned breadcrumbs

Directions:

1. Preheat oven to 350 degrees F.
2. Combine all the ingredients except the breadcrumbs in a large bowl. Transfer to a 3 quart casserole dish.
3. Bake for 30 minutes. Remove from oven and top with the breadcrumbs.
4. Bake for 10 minutes more, until top is browned and casserole is bubbly.

Creamy Chicken, Broccoli, and Rice
Serves 6

Ingredients:

1 can condensed cream of broccoli or cheddar cheese soup
1 cup water
1 package frozen broccoli
1 6-ounce package seasoned wild rice mix
6 boneless, skinless chicken breasts
1 cup shredded cheddar cheese

Directions:

1. Preheat oven to 350 degrees F.
2. Combine the soup, water, rice, and seasoning packet, broccoli and cheese in a 3 quart casserole dish.
3. Lay the chicken breasts on top. Cover with foil and bake for 1 hour, or until chicken is cooked through.

Creamy Tetrazzini

Serves 6

Ingredients:

1 can condensed cream of mushroom soup
1 cup milk
1 cup grated Parmesan cheese
1 packet Lipton onion soup (MS3)
2 cups chopped or shredded cooked chicken (TS2)
4 cups cooked egg noodles
1/2 cup seasoned breadcrumbs
2 tablespoons melted butter

Directions:

1. Preheat oven to 375 degrees F.
2. Combine the soup, milk, cheese, and onion soup mix in a large bowl. Add the chicken, mushrooms and egg noodles. Toss them well and add to a 3-quart baking dish.
3. Mix the breadcrumbs with the butter and sprinkle over the casserole. Bake for 25-30 minutes, or until the mixture is hot, bubbling, and lightly browned.

Fiesta Chicken and Rice
Serves 6

Ingredients:

1 can condensed cream of chicken soup
1 cup water
1 cup prepared salsa
1 cup uncooked white rice
1 can corn kernels, drained
6 boneless, skinless chicken breasts
1 cup shredded cheddar or Mexican style cheese

Directions:

1. Preheat oven to 350 degrees F.
2. Combine the soup, salsa, rice, and corn in a medium bowl.
3. Spread in a 2 quart casserole dish. Top with the chicken breasts. Cover with foil and bake for 45 minutes. Remove from oven and top with cheese.
4. Bake for 15 more minutes, until cheese is melted and bubbly and chicken is cooked through.

Quick and Easy Beef Dinners

Beef is a staple protein for many families, and it's easy to prepare and delicious to eat. Luckily there are plenty of ways to enjoy it in everything from casseroles to tacos to pasta dishes, and you'll find a little bit of everything in this section.

If you want to make your beef dinners even easier, check out the shortcuts and substitution page in this book. There, you'll learn how to get your beef ready to go so that getting dinner on the table is even easier than you ever thought possible. From there, you and your family can enjoy a home cooked meal every night of the week. While your family will think you've slaved away to get them dinner, it will be our little secret how you really did it!

Skillet Pasta & Beef Dinner
Serves 4

Ingredients:

1 pound lean ground beef
One 24 ounce jar pasta sauce
2 cups hot water
2 cups uncooked rotini pasta
1 cup shredded mozzarella cheese (about 4 oz.)
1 teaspoon seasoned salt
1/2 teaspoon garlic powder

Directions:

1. Place ground beef in a large skillet with a cover.
2. Add 2 cups of hot water and jar of pasta sauce and salt and garlic powder.
3. Bring to a boil over high heat, stirring to break up ground beef.
4. Stir in uncooked rotini, reduce heat to medium and cook covered, stirring occasionally, 15 minutes or until rotini is tender.
5. Remove from heat, sprinkle with cheese. Cover and let stand until cheese is melted.

Oven Tacos
Serves 4-6

Ingredients:

1 1/2 cups precooked ground beef
1 can refried beans
1 package taco seasoning
12 prepared taco shells
1 cup shredded cheese

Directions:

1. Preheat oven to 350 degrees F.
2. Mix together beef, beans and seasoning.
3. Divide mixture between 12 shells, filling and standing up in 9 x 13 pan.
4. Sprinkle cheese over tacos, making sure it gets inside each taco.
5. Bake for 15 to 20 minutes until filling is heated thru and cheese is melted.
6. Serve with shredded lettuce, tomato, olives, sour cream, guacamole or other desired toppings.

Baked Porcupine Meatballs
Serves 4 to 6

A little more work but so worth it...let the kids roll the meatballs

Ingredients:

1 1/2 pound lean ground beef
2/3 cup long-grain rice, uncooked
1/2 cup water
1/2 envelope Lipton onion soup mix (1 heaping tablespoon)
or 1/4 cup finely chopped onion
1 teaspoon seasoned salt
1/4 teaspoon garlic powder
1/8 teaspoon pepper

Topping:
1 large can (15 ounces) tomato sauce
1 cup water
2 teaspoons Worcestershire sauce

Directions:

1. Preheat oven to 350 degrees F.
2. Mix ground beef with rice, 1/2 cup of water, chopped onion, seasoned salt, garlic powder, and pepper. Save dishes and do this in the pan.
3. Shape porcupine ground beef mixture by tablespoon into 1 1/2-inch balls, and place into ungreased 9 x 13 baking dish. You can also press mixture into bottom of pan and using a spatula, separate into squares, leaving about ½ inch between the rows. Meat squares taste the same as meatballs but don't roll off the plate as easily.
4. Mix the remaining ingredients and pour over the porcupine meatballs.
5. Bake in oven for about 45 minutes. Uncover and bake porcupine meatballs 15 to 20 minutes longer.

Beefy Biscuit Bake
Serves 4-6

Ingredients:

1 1/2 pounds cooked ground beef
1/2 envelope Lipton Onion Soup mix (about 1 heaping Tablespoon)
1 8 ounce package cream cheese, softened
1 can Cream of Mushroom soup
1/4 cup milk
1/4 cup sliced ripe olives (optional)
1 small can mushrooms, drained (optional)
1/2 teaspoon seasoned salt
1/4 teaspoon pepper
1 7 ounce can biscuits
Melted butter
Parmesan cheese

Directions:

1. Preheat oven to 375 degrees F.
2. Spray a 2 quart casserole dish with nonstick spray.
3. Mix soup, cream cheese, milk, onion soup mix, salt and pepper in casserole until smooth.
4. Add ground beef, olives and/or mushrooms and stir to blend.
5. Bake for 30 minutes until hot and bubbly.
6. Arrange biscuits on top, return to oven and bake 10 to 15 minutes until biscuits are browned. Brush biscuits with melted butter and sprinkle lightly with parmesan cheese if desired.

Tip: Add a 16-ounce bag of frozen vegetables like peas and carrots and add to meat mixture before baking if desired.

Easiest Meatloaf Ever
Serves 6-8

Ingredients:

1 1/2 pounds ground meat, beef or turkey or mixture of 2
1 cup water
1 egg
1 box Stove Top Stuffing Mix (unprepared)

Directions:

1. Preheat oven to 350 degrees F.
2. Spray 9 x 13 baking pan with nonstick spray.
3. Break meat apart into chunks and drop in pan. Add egg to water and blend with a fork.
4. Add stuffing mix and egg water to pan, blend together with hands or large fork or spatula. (As my granddaughter says, "smoosh" it together).After mixing, form into a loaf in the center of pan.
5. Bake for 45 minutes.

Easy Oven Cheeseburger Sliders
Serves 12

No frying, no guessing, cut these burgers to size AFTER they cook!

Ingredients:

1 1/2 pounds lean ground beef
1/4 cup bread or cracker crumbs
1/2 package Lipton Onion Soup mix (about 1 heaping tablespoon)
3-4 slices cheese
1 package (12 count) Kings Hawaiian Dinner Rolls, or slider buns

Directions:

1. Preheat oven to 400 degrees F.
2. Place beef, crumbs and soup mix in 9 x 13 pan, then mix together and press into single layer covering the bottom of pan.
1. Use a fork to poke holes thru meat.
2. Bake for 30 minutes. Meat will shrink away from the side of the pan.
6. Hold meat in place with a spatula, drain away liquid into disposable container, then cover with layer of cheese and return to oven until cheese is melted.
7. Remove from oven and cut into 12 squares.
8. Place on buns and serve with desired toppings such as lettuce, tomato, pickle, etc.

Cheesy Mexican Beef Skillet Dinner
Serves 4

Ingredients:

1 pound 90% lean ground beef
2 cups water
1 16-ounce jar your favorite salsa
1 7-ounce box macaroni and cheese (Kraft is a favorite at my house!)
1 can black beans , drained
1 can corn , drained
1 cup shredded cheese

Directions:

1. Heat a large skillet over medium heat. Add the ground beef and water and cook until browned.
2. Add the macaroni, cheese packet, and salsa. Cover and cook for about 10 minutes, until the pasta is tender and cooked.
3. Uncover and stir in the beans and corn. Stir until heated, top with the shredded cheese and serve.

Tip: This is delicious when topped with some sour cream and green onions. Additional salsa is a delicious addition as well.

Classic Italian Pasta Dinner

Serves 6

Ingredients:

1 pound 90% lean ground beef
1 cup chopped onion (TS3)
1 teaspoon garlic powder
1 teaspoon Italian seasoning
3 cups uncooked pasta, such as penne or rigatoni
3 cups water
1 32-ounce jar your favorite pasta sauce
2 cups shredded mozzarella cheese

Directions:

1. Heat a large saucepot over medium heat. Add the ground beef, onions, garlic powder and Italian seasoning. Cook until beef is no longer pink.
2. Add the pasta, water, and sauce. Cook for about 15 minutes, until pasta is cooked through.
3. Top with cheese and serve.

Tip: My family loves garlic bread, and this dish is perfect for it. Grab your favorite frozen loaf at the grocery store, and pop it in the over after you've added the pasta and sauce. While your meal simmers, your garlic bread bakes. Everything will be done about the same time for a delicious meal everyone will love.

Meatloaf and Mashed Potato Muffins
Serves 6

Ingredients:

1 pound ground beef
1 package stuffing mix
1 packet Lipton onion soup (MS3)
1 cup water
1 egg
1 package instant mashed potatoes, prepared according to the package directions (My family's favorite is Idahoan Baby Reds)
1 12 ounce jar of beef gravy, warmed

Directions:

1. Preheat oven to 350 degrees F. Lightly spray a 12 cup muffin pan with cooking spray.
2. In a large bowl, combine the ground beef, stuffing mix, water and egg. Using your hands, mix it well, but don't over mix!
3. Divide the meatloaf mixture into the muffin tins. Bake for 25-30 minutes, until tops are browned and meatloaf is cooked through.
4. While the meatloaf is baking, prepare your mashed potatoes, and warm your gravy.
5. Scoop the mashed potatoes over the meat loaf muffins and serve with the gravy. When served with steamed broccoli or your favorite vegetable, this becomes a complete meal that everyone will enjoy!

Amazingly Easy and Delicious Enchiladas

Serves 4

Ingredients:

1 pound ground beef (TS1)
1 16-ounce jar your favorite salsa
2 cups shredded cheese (a Mexican blend is our favorite, but cheddar works nicely too!)
12 corn or flour tortillas (corn are more authentic, but flour are easier to work with)

Directions:

1. Preheat oven to 350 degrees F.
2. Heat a skillet over medium heat and add the beef. When cooked through, stir in half the salsa and half the cheese. Stir until heated and cheese is melted.
3. Pour half of the remaining salsa in the bottom of a large casserole dish.
4. Spoon some of the beef filling down the center of each tortilla (if using corn, you'll need to heat them in the microwave first to make them more pliable) and lay seam side down in the casserole dish. When all tortillas are filled, top with remaining salsa and cheese.
5. Bake for 15-20 minutes, until cheese is melted.

One Skillet Cheesy Beef Stroganoff
Serves 6

Ingredients:

1 pound ground beef (TS1)
2 cups water
4 cups uncooked egg noodles
1/2 pound Velveeta, cubed
1 can condensed cream of mushroom soup
1 teaspoon Lawry's seasoned salt

Directions:

1. Heat a large skillet over medium heat. Add the ground beef and cook until it's no longer pink. Drain.
2. Add water to the beef. Bring to a boil and add the egg noodles. Cover and cook on low heat for 8-10 minutes, until noodles are cooked and tender.
3. Add the cheese, mushroom soup, and Lawry's and stir until melted and creamy. Serve.

Mexican Pizza
Serves 4-6

Ingredients:

1 pound ground beef
1 packet taco seasoning (MS1)
1 12-inch prepared pizza crust
2 cups shredded Mexican cheese
1 cup shredded lettuce
1 cup crushed tortilla chips
1 cup prepared salsa

Directions:

1. Preheat oven to 400 degrees F.
2. Heat a large skillet to medium heat. Add the ground beef and the taco seasoning and cook until no longer pink.
3. Lay the pizza crust on a baking sheet and spread the ground beef over the crust. Top with cheese and bake for 10 minutes, until cheese is melted.
4. Remove from oven, top with lettuce and crushed tortilla ships. Serve with the salsa.

Southwest Sloppy Joes
Serves 6

Ingredients:

1 pound ground beef
1 cup chopped onions (TS3)
2 cans Rotel tomatoes, with juices
1 packet taco seasoning (MS1)
1 can corn, drained
1 cup shredded Mexican style cheese
6 sandwich buns, for serving

Directions:

1. Heat a large skillet over medium heat. Add the ground beef and onions and cook until beef is no longer pink.
2. Add the tomatoes, taco seasoning and corn and simmer for 10-15 minutes, until sauce is thickened.
3. Stir in the cheese and stir until melted and heated through.
4. Serve on the sandwich buns.

Cheeseburger Meatloaf
Serves 8-10

Ingredients:

1 pound ground beef
12 crackers (Ritz or Saltine crackers work well), finely crushed
2 tablespoons mustard
1 egg
1/4 cup ketchup
4 slices American cheese

Directions:

1. Preheat oven to 350 degrees F.
2. Combine the beef, crushed crackers, mustard and egg in a large bowl. Mix with your hands until well combined.
3. Put the mixture in a standard loaf pan. Bake for 45 minutes.
4. Remove from oven and top with the ketchup. Lay the cheese slices on top and bake for 5 more minutes, until cheese is melted and serve.

Skillet Lasagna
Serves 4

Ingredients:

1 pound ground beef
1 packet Italian dressing seasoning (MS8)
2 cups water
2 cups uncooked pasta, such as penne or bow ties
1 28-ounce jar your favorite pasta sauce
1/2 cup ricotta cheese
1 cup shredded mozzarella cheese

Directions:

1. Heat a medium skillet over medium heat. Add the ground beef and Italian dressing packet. Cook until beef is no longer pink.
2. Add the water and pasta. Bring to a boil and reduce heat to medium low. Cover and cook for 10 minutes, until pasta is tender.
3. Add the sauce, stir in cheeses and heat through. Serve.

Asian Lettuce Wraps
Serves 4

Ingredients:

1 pound ground beef
1/2 cup chopped onion (TS3)
1/2 teaspoon garlic powder
1/2 cup prepared Asian dressing
1 cup shredded cabbage
1 head Iceberg lettuce, leaves left in tact

Directions:

1. Heat a large skillet over medium heat. Add the beef, onions, and garlic powder and cook until beef is no longer pink.
2. Add the dressing and shredded cabbage and cook until cabbage is soft.
3. To serve, spoon the beef mixture into the lettuce leaves.

Italian Pot Roast
Serves 6-8

Ingredients:

1 3-4 pound pot roast
1 packet Italian dressing seasoning (MS8)
2 tablespoons vegetable oil
1 can diced tomatoes, undrained
2 cups chicken or beef stock (TS4)
3 large potatoes, peeled and cut into bite sized pieces
2 onions, quartered

Directions:

1. Preheat oven to 300 degrees F. Season the roast with the Italian dressing mix, making sure to cover the entire roast liberally.
2. Heat a large Dutch oven or ovenproof pot over medium high heat. Add the vegetable oil and the roast. Sear the roast on all sides until browned. Add the tomatoes, stock, and vegetables.
3. Cover and put in the oven. Cook the roast for 3-4 hours, until it is tender and falls apart easily with a fork. Serve the roast with the vegetables.

Nacho Skillet

Serves 4

Ingredients:

1 pound ground beef
1 cup chopped onion (TS3)
1/2 packet taco seasoning (MS1)
1/2 cup water
1 can condensed nacho cheese soup
1 tomato, diced
2 cups shredded lettuce
1 cup broken tortilla chips or corn chips

Directions:

1. Heat a large skillet over medium heat. Add the ground beef and the onion and cook until beef is no longer pink in the center. Add the taco seasoning, stir and add the water and nacho soup.
2. Top with the tomatoes, lettuce, and corn chips.

Tip: Serve this with your favorite salsa and sour cream, and it's better than any nachos you'll get in a restaurant!

Quick and Easy Steak Fajitas
Serves 6

Ingredients:

1 tablespoon vegetable oil
1 pound steak, sliced into strips
1 packet fajita seasoning mix
1 bag frozen pepper and onion mix
12 large tortillas, warmed

Directions:

1. Heat a large skillet over medium heat. Add the vegetable oil and the steak. Sear until steak is browned on all sides.
2. Add half the fajita seasoning and stir until well coated. Remove the steak from the pan and set aside. Add the veggies and the rest of the seasoning.
3. Stir and cook until veggies are crisp tender. Add the steak back into the pan and stir until heated through. Serve with the tortillas.

Tip: Fajitas are a restaurant favorite, but they are expensive. To recreate a restaurant meal, I serve these with lots of shredded, cheese, sour cream, and guacamole. It's easy for everyone to customize his or her own meal, and we save money at that!

Stroganoff Pot Pie
Serves 4

Ingredients:

1 pound ground beef (TS1)
2 cups water
1 can condensed cream of mushroom soup
2 cups frozen mixed vegetables (A mix of corn, carrots, and peas is a favorite in my house, but feel free to use your own favorites!)
1 ready-made piecrust
1 egg, beaten

Directions:

1. Preheat oven to 400 degrees F.
2. Heat a large skillet over medium heat. Add the ground beef and cook until no longer pink. Add the water, soup, and veggies. Stir until well combined.
3. Spread mixture into a 9-inch pie plate. Top with the pre-rolled crust. Press the edges to the dish.
4. Using a sharp knife, make a few slashes in the crust to vent. Brush with the egg.
5. Bake for 30-35 minutes, until crust is browned and pie is bubbly.

Beef and Cabbage Crescent Rolls
Serves 6-8

Ingredients:

1 pound ground beef
1 packet Lipton onion soup (MS3)
2 cups shredded cabbage
1/2 cup shredded cheddar cheese
2 cans refrigerated crescent rolls

Directions:

1. Preheat oven to 400 degrees F.
2. Heat a large skillet over medium heat. Add the ground beef and onion soup mix and stir until beef is no longer pink. Stir in the cabbage.
3. Cook until cabbage is soft and stir in the cheese. Stir until cheese is melted.
4. Open the crescent rolls and spray a large baking sheet with cooking spray.
5. Fill each roll with a few tablespoons of the beef mixture, and roll up, sealing the edges. Lay on the baking sheet.
6. Bake for 12-15 minutes, until rolls are browned.

Tip: These make excellent appetizers, but sometimes I like to serve them with a big green salad for a full meal. They're filling, and everyone in the family loves them!

Beef Stew in a Bread Bowl
Serves 6

Ingredients:

1 tablespoon vegetable oil
1 pound boneless sirloin, cut into bite sized pieces
1 packet Lipton onion soup (MS3)
1/2 packet brown gravy mix (MS5)
1 large potato, peeled and diced
1 can diced tomatoes, undrained
2 cups water
2 cups baby carrots
2 cups frozen peas
1 can large biscuits (I like Pillsbury Grand!)

1. Preheat oven to 350 degrees F. Lightly spray a large muffin tin with cooking spray.
2. Heat the vegetable oil in a large pot or Dutch oven. Add the steak and cook until browned on all sides.
3. Add the onion soup, gravy, potatoes, tomatoes, water, and vegetables. Bring to a boil and reduce heat. Simmer while you prepare the bread bowls.
4. Open the biscuits and flatten them to about 1/4 inch thick. Lay one in each muffin tin and form a bowl, pushing the bread up until you have a slight rim. Save extra biscuits for another use.
5. Spoon the beef stew into the bread cups. Cover with foil and bake for 10 minutes.
6. Uncover and bake for 10 more minutes, or until bread bowls are browned and stew is bubbly.

Spicy Beef and Rice Skillet Dinner
Serves 6

Ingredients:

4 strips bacon, diced
1 pound ground beef
1 cup chopped onion (TS3)
1 cup chopped bell pepper
1 teaspoon garlic powder
1 tablespoon chili powder
2 cups water
1 can diced tomatoes
2 cups instant white rice, uncooked
1 cup shredded cheddar cheese

Directions:

1. Heat a large skillet over medium heat. Add the bacon and cook until crisp. Add the beef, onions, and peppers and cook until beef is no longer pink in the center.
2. Add the garlic powder, chili powder, water, tomatoes and rice. Stir and bring to a boil.
3. Reduce heat to low and cover. Simmer for 6-7 minutes, until rice is tender. Uncover and top with the cheese. Serve when cheese is melted.

Beefy Shells and Cheese
Serves 4

12 large pasta shells, cooked according to the directions on the box
1/2 pound ground beef (TS1)
1/2 cup cottage cheese
1 cup shredded mozzarella cheese
1/2 cup grated Parmesan cheese
1 egg
1 12-ounce jar pasta sauce

Directions:

1. Preheat oven to 350 degrees F.
2. Heat a large skillet over medium heat. Add the beef and cook until no longer pink in the center. Drain. Add to a large bowl.
3. Add the cottage cheese, half the mozzarella cheese, and Parmesan to the beef. Stir and add the egg.
4. Pour half the pasta sauce in a large casserole dish. Fill each cooked shell with the beef mixture and lay in the dish. Pour remaining sauce overtop and top with remaining cheese.
5. Cover with foil and bake for 45 minutes, until bubbly.

Shredded Beef Tacos
Serves 6

Ingredients:

1 packet taco seasoning (MS1)
1 3-4 pound chuck roast
1 tablespoon vegetable oil
1 can Rotel tomatoes, undrained
2 cups chicken or beef stock (TS4)
12 soft or hard taco shells
Shredded lettuce, salsa, and shredded cheese for serving

Directions:

1. Preheat oven to 300 degrees F.
2. Season the roast with the taco season until well coated.
3. Heat a large Dutch oven or pot over medium high heat. Add the vegetable oil and the roast and sear until browned on all sides. Add the tomatoes and stock.
4. Cover and put in the oven. Cook for 3-4 hours, until meat is tender and shreds easily with a fork.
5. Before serving, warm the taco shells according to the package directions.
6. Serve the beef in the shells, topped with lettuce, cheese, and salsa.

Southwest Beef and Noodles
Serves 6

Ingredients:

1 pound ground beef
2 cups egg noodles, uncooked
1 can corn, drained
1 cup water
1/2 cup prepared salsa
1 16-ounce can tomato sauce

Directions:

1. Heat a large skillet over medium heat. Add ground beef and cook until no longer pink. Add the noodles, corn, water, salsa, and tomato sauce. Bring to a boil.
2. Reduce heat to low and cover. Cook for 10 minutes, or until noodles are tender. Serve.

Delicious Chicken Dishes

In my household, chicken is king when it comes to quick and easy dinners that are mouthwateringly delicious. It's an easy and inexpensive protein that everyone loves and goes with just about anything.

Whether you're looking for party favorites, or classic dishes, you'll find a little bit of everything in this section. You'll be surprised at how easy some of these dishes are, since they taste as if you slaved all day in the kitchen. These are my favorite types of meals, and once you try them, they'll be your favorites as well!

Chicken and Mini Dumplings
Serves 4

Ingredients:

4 Boneless, skinless chicken breasts
1 can Cream of Chicken soup
1 Small Onion, chopped
3/4 cup celery, chopped (about 3 ribs)
1 egg
1/2 teaspoon poultry seasoning
1/2 teaspoon salt
1/4 teaspoon pepper
1 tube refrigerator biscuits (7 ounce)

Directions:

1. Preheat oven to 350 degrees F.
2. Place chicken pieces (I like to cut them in half) in a 9x13 pan sprayed with nonstick spray. In a bowl, combine soup, celery, onion, egg and seasonings.
3. Mix until blended.
4. Cut each biscuit into 8 or 10 small pieces, then add to bowl and stir gently.
5. Pour sauce evenly over chicken.
6. Bake for about 1 hour, until chicken is done and biscuit pieces have puffed and browned.

Roasted Chicken and Vegetable Dinner
Serves 4-6

Ingredients:

2 pounds bone-in chicken pieces, whatever your favorites are
1 pound baby red potatoes
1/2 pound baby carrots
1 onion, sliced
1 tablespoon vegetable oil
1 teaspoon Mrs. Dash
1 teaspoon Morton's Nature seasoning

Directions:

1. Preheat oven to 375 degrees F. Spray a 9x13 casserole dish with cooking spray.
2. Lay the chicken and vegetables in prepared dish. Add the rest of the ingredients and stir well to coat.
3. Bake for 1 hour and check the chicken for doneness. Continue roasting until chicken is cooked through and vegetables are tender.

Tip: Don't limit yourself to just the vegetables listed here. You can use any root vegetable you have on hand. I've used sweet potatoes, turnips, and beets with much success. You can even use softer vegetables if that's what you like or have; just throw them in about halfway through the cooking process so that they don't get overcooked.

Easy Peasy Chicken and Rice
Serves 4

Ingredients:

4 boneless, skinless chicken breasts, cut in quarters
2 cups frozen peas
1 cup uncooked white rice (not instant)
1 can cream soup, chicken, mushroom, celery (Your choice)
1 envelope Lipton onion soup mix
2 cups hot water

Directions:

1. Preheat oven to 375 degrees F.
2. Nonstick spray a 2 quart casserole dish with a lid.
3. Put rice, both soups, water, and peas in casserole and blend with spoon or whisk.
4. Add chicken pieces and stir together.
5. Cover and bake 1 hour until rice has absorbed water and chicken is cooked through.

Oh So Easy Chicken Dinner
Serves 4-6

Ingredients:

4-6 boneless, skinless chicken breasts
1-2 cans green beans
2-3 potatoes, cubed
1 packet Good Seasons Italian Dressing Mix
1 stick butter, melted with 1 teaspoon Lawry's Seasoned Salt

Directions:

1. Spray a 9" x 13" dish with cooking spray.
2. Empty one or two cans of drained green beans down one side of the baking dish
3. Place chicken breasts in the middle of the dish in a line
4. Put cut potatoes on the third side of the dish.
5. Drizzle melted butter over the top of everything.
6. Sprinkle dry Italian Dressing Mix over the entire dish. Cover with foil and bake at 350 degrees for one hour, removing foil for last 15 minutes
7. Remove from oven, and serve.

Baked Chicken Fajitas
Serves 4

Ingredients:

1 pound boneless, skinless chicken breasts, cut into strips
1 (15 ounce) can diced tomatoes
1 (4 ounce) can diced green chilies
1 medium onion, cut in thin strips
1 large bell pepper, or 1 small green and 1 small red pepper,
seeded and cut in thin strips
2 tablespoons vegetable oil
1 package fajita seasoning mix OR
2 teaspoons chili powder
2 teaspoons cumin
1/2 teaspoon garlic powder
1/2 teaspoon dried oregano
1/4 teaspoon salt
12 flour tortillas, warmed to serve

Directions:

1. Preheat the oven to 400 degrees.
2. Grease a 9x13 baking dish.
3. Mix together chicken, tomatoes, chilies, peppers, and onions in the dish.
4. In a small bowl combine the oil and Fajita Mix OR spices.
5. Drizzle the spice mixture over the chicken and toss to coat.
6. Bake uncovered for 20-25 minutes or until chicken is cooked through and the vegetables are tender.
7. Serve with warmed tortillas. Offer sour cream, guacamole and shredded cheese for garnish.

One Pot Creamy Alfredo Chicken Pasta
Serves 4

Ingredients:

3 tablespoons vegetable oil
1 pound boneless, skinless chicken breasts, sliced
1 teaspoon garlic powder
1/2 teaspoon Mrs. Dash
2 cups chicken broth
2 5-ounce cans evaporated milk
1/2 pound penne pasta (or whatever your favorite is)
2 cups grated Parmesan cheese

Directions:

1. Heat a large skillet over medium heat and add the oil and chicken. Cook until it's lightly browned and add the garlic powder and Mrs. Dash.
2. Add the chicken broth, evaporated milk, and pasta.
3. Stir, bring to a boil and then reduce heat. Cover and simmer for 15-20 minutes, until pasta is cooked. Uncover and stir in the cheese.

Italian Stuffed Chicken Breasts
Serves 4

Ingredients:

4 boneless, skinless chicken breasts
1 bunch basil leaves
4 slices mozzarella cheese
4 sun dried tomatoes
4 tablespoons Balsamic Vinaigrette salad dressing

Directions:

1. Preheat oven to 350 degrees F.
2. Make a cut in the side of each chicken breast. Insert 1 or 2 basil leaves, a slice of cheese, and a sun dried tomato into each.
3. Lay the chicken breasts on a baking sheet and brush with a tablespoons dressing.
4. Bake 30-45 minutes until chicken is cooked through. Serve with vegetable and side of your choice.

Tip: Looking for an easy side? Wrap a small baked potato in foil and pop it in the oven. By the time your meal is done, you've got a side with no extra effort!

Creamy Bacon and Onion Smothered Chicken Breasts

Serves 4

Ingredients:

5 slices bacon, chopped
1 cup chopped onion (TS3)
1 packet Lipton onion soup (MS3)
4 boneless, skinless chicken breasts, sliced
1 can evaporated milk
Egg noodles or rice, for serving

Directions:

1. Heat a large skillet over medium heat. Add the bacon and onion and cook until bacon is crisp.
2. Add the onion soup and sliced chicken and cook until chicken is browned and cooked through.
3. Add the evaporated milk and stir to coat the chicken. When heated through, serve the chicken topped with the sauce. Serve over rice or noodles.

Easy Chicken Milanese
Serves 6

Ingredients:

1/2 cup mayonnaise
1 teaspoon garlic powder
6 boneless, skinless chicken breasts
1 cup crushed crackers, such as Ritz
2 tablespoons dried parsley
2 tablespoons vegetable oil

Directions:

1. Combine the mayo with the garlic powder in a bowl and coat the chicken breasts with the mixture.
2. Combine the cracker crumbs and the parsley in a shallow dish or pie plate. Dredge the chicken in the crumbs until thoroughly coated on all sides.
3. Heat the oil in a medium skillet. Cook the chicken until browned and crispy on both sides and cooked through. Serve with vegetables and sides of your choice.

Sweet and Sour Chicken in a Skillet
Serves 4

Ingredients:

1 tablespoon vegetable oil
1 pound chicken breasts, cubed
1 cup sliced onion (TS3)
1 bag frozen mixed vegetables of your choice (I like peppers, broccoli, and carrots)
1/2 cup Catalina salad dressing
1/2 cup brown sugar
1 tablespoon cornstarch
1/4 cup soy sauce
1 can pineapple chunks with liquid
Cooked rice, for serving (TS8)

Directions:

1. Heat a large skillet over medium high heat. Add the vegetable oil and the chicken. Cook until chicken is browned and add the onion and frozen vegetables. Stir.
2. Combine the dressing, sugar, cornstarch and soy sauce in a small bowl. Add it to the skillet along with the pineapple. Stir and cook for 1 minute, until sauce is thickened. Serve with the rice.

Cheesy Chicken Spaghetti
Serves 6

Ingredients:

1/2 pound uncooked spaghetti noodles (TS8)
1 tablespoon vegetable oil
1 pound boneless chicken breasts, cubed
1 package Velveeta, cubed
1 can condensed cream of chicken soup
1 small can sliced mushrooms, drained
1/2 cup milk

Directions:

1. Cook the spaghetti according to the package directions.
2. Heat a large skillet over medium heat and add the vegetable oil. Add the chicken pieces and cook until browned and cooked through. Add the cheese and mushrooms. Stir until cheese is melted and add the soup and mushrooms. Stir.
3. Add the cooked spaghetti and stir until well combined and heated through. Serve.

Fiesta Style Chicken in Cheese Sauce
Serves 6

Ingredients:

5 slices bacon, chopped
1 cup chopped onion(TS3)
1/2 packet taco seasoning (MS1)
4 boneless, skinless chicken breasts
1 can condensed nacho cheese soup
1 cup milk
Rice, for serving (TS8)

Directions:

1. Heat a large skillet over medium heat. Add the bacon and onion and cook until bacon is crisp. Add the taco seasoning, stir, and add the chicken breasts. Cook until the chicken is browned on both sides and cooked through.
2. Add the nacho soup and milk. Stir to coat the chicken. When heated through, serve with the rice.

Tuscan Chicken and Broccoli
Serves 4

Ingredients:

2 cups penne or bow tie pasta, uncooked (TS8)
1 bag frozen broccoli florets
1 tablespoons olive oil
4 boneless, skinless chicken breasts, cubed
1 cup shredded mozzarella cheese
1/4 cup Italian dressing
1/2 cup chicken stock (TS4)
1/4 tablespoon grated Parmesan cheese

Directions:

1. Bring a large pot of water to a boil. Add the pasta and cook according to the package directions. Three to four minutes before pasta is done, add the broccoli to the pot. Drain.
2. Heat a large skillet over medium heat. Add the olive oil and chicken pieces, and cook until done. Add the salad dressing and stock to the pan and stir. Add the pasta and broccoli and serve when heated through.

Chicken Fajita Skillet Dinner
Serves 4

Ingredients:

1 tablespoon vegetable oil
1 pound chicken breast, cut into strips
1 package fajita seasoning
1 package frozen peppers and onions
1 1/2 cups instant white rice
1 cup water
1 cup shredded Mexican style cheese

Directions:

1. Heat a large skillet over medium heat. Add the vegetable oil and chicken breasts. Cook until chicken is browned all over.
2. Add the fajita seasoning and peppers. Stir and add the rice and water. Bring to a boil and reduce heat. Simmer for 20 minutes.
3. Add cheese and stir until heated through.

Crispy Pesto Chicken
Serves 4

Ingredients:

4 boneless, skinless chicken breasts
1/2 cup prepared pesto
1 cup Italian seasoned bread crumbs
1/2 cup shredded mozzarella cheese

Directions:

1. Preheat oven to 350 degrees F.
2. Coat the chicken in the pesto. Put the breadcrumbs in a shallow pan. Dredge the chicken in the breadcrumbs. Lay on a baking sheet.
3. Bake for 25-30 minutes until chicken is cooked through. Remove from oven and top with the cheese. Bake for 5 minutes until cheese is melted and serve.

Baked Chicken Cordon Bleu
Serves 6

Ingredients:

1 box seasoned stuffing mix, prepared as directed on package
6 boneless, skinless chicken breasts
6 slices smoked ham
1 can condensed cream of chicken soup
1 tablespoon honey mustard
6 slices Swiss cheese

Directions:

1. Preheat oven to 350 degrees F.
2. Lay the chicken breasts in a baking dish. Lay a slice of ham on each.
3. Combine the soup with the honey mustard and top the chicken with the stuffing.
4. Lay a slice of Swiss cheese on each breast. Cover dish with foil.
5. Bake for 30-35 minutes until chicken is cooked through.

Cheesy Chicken Pot Pie
Serves 8

Ingredients:

1 tablespoon vegetable oil
1 pound boneless, skinless chicken breasts, cubed
1 packet Italian dressing seasoning (MS8)
2 cups frozen vegetables (I like a mixture of peas, carrots, and green beans)
1 can condensed cream of chicken soup
1/2 pound Velveeta, cubed
1 prepared piecrust (I like Pillsbury)

Directions:

1. Preheat oven to 350 degrees F.
2. Heat a large skillet over medium heat. Add the vegetable oil and chicken and cook until chicken is browned on all sides. Add the Italian dressing packet and vegetables and stir.
3. Add the soup and Velveeta and stir until cheese is melted. Transfer to a deep 9 inch pie plate. Top with the crust and seal the edges. Cut a few slits in the pie crust.
4. Bake for 30-40 minutes until crust is golden brown. Allow to rest for 5-10 minutes before slicing and serving.

One Pan Chicken and Dumplings

Serves 4

Ingredients:

1 tablespoon vegetable oil
1 pound boneless, skinless chicken breasts, cubed
1 packet Italian dressing seasoning (MS8)
2 cups frozen vegetables (I like a mixture of peas, carrots, and green beans)
1 can condensed cream of chicken soup
1 cup chicken stock (TS4)
1 can refrigerated biscuits, each cut in half

Directions:

1. Heat a large skillet with lid over medium heat. Add the vegetable oil and chicken pieces and cook until chicken is browned on all sides. Add the seasoning and vegetables. Stir.
2. Add the soup and chicken stock and bring to a boil. Reduce heat.
3. Drop the biscuits in the pan, keeping them separated. Cover and cook for 20 minutes over low heat, until chicken is done.

Easy Chicken Cacciatore
Serves 6

Ingredients:

1/2 cup Italian dressing
3 pounds chicken thighs and drumsticks
1 small can sliced mushrooms, drained
1 bag frozen onions and peppers
1 can diced tomatoes, with garlic
Rice, for serving

Directions:

1. Heat a skillet over medium heat and add the Italian dressing. Add the chicken and cook until browned on all sides. Add the mushrooms, frozen vegetables and tomatoes.
2. Turn heat down to low and cover. Simmer for 30 minutes, until chicken is cooked through. Serve over the rice.

Chicken, Bacon, and Ranch Pizza
Serves 6

Ingredients:

1 refrigerated pizza crust
1/4 cup mayonnaise
1/2 cup Ranch dressing
2 cups shredded cheddar cheese
2 cups chopped or shredded cooked chicken (TS2)
6 slices bacon, cooked and crumbled (TS6)
2 cups shredded lettuce
1 tomato, chopped

Directions:

1. Preheat oven to 400 degrees F. Spray a baking pan with cooking spray.
2. Unroll the pizza crust and lay on the baking pan.
3. Combine the mayo with half of the dressing and spread over the pizza crust. Top with the chicken, followed by the cheese and bacon.
4. Bake for 10-15 minutes, until cheese is melted and crust is browned.
5. Top with the lettuce, tomatoes, and leftover dressing.

Chicken with Creamy Bacon Sauce
Serves 4

Ingredients:

4 slices bacon, chopped
1 pound chicken breasts, cubed
1/2 package cream cheese
1/2 cup chicken stock (TS4)
Pasta or rice, for serving (TS8)

Directions:

1. Heat a large skillet over medium high heat. Add the bacon and cook until crisp. Add the chicken and cook until browned on all sides and cooked through.
2. Add the cream cheese and stir until melted. Stir in the chicken stock. Stir until creamy.
3. Serve the chicken over either pasta or rice for a complete meal.

Island Chicken
Serves 4

Ingredients:

1 tablespoon vegetable oil
1 pound chicken breast, cubed
1/2 cup orange juice
1/2 cup canned pineapple chunks
1/4 cup Asian Sesame dressing
Rice, for serving (TS8)

Directions:

1. Heat a large skillet over medium heat. Add the vegetable oil and chicken breast. Cook until chicken is browned and cooked through.
2. Add the orange juice and pineapple chunks, stir and add the dressing.
3. When heated through, serve over rice.

Lemony Chicken and Noodles
Serves 4

Ingredients:

3 cups uncooked egg noodles
1/2 cup Italian dressing
Zest and juice of 1 lemon
4 boneless skinless chicken breasts
1 small can sliced mushrooms
1 bag frozen onions and peppers

Directions:

1. Cook the egg noodles according to the directions on the package.
2. Combine the dressing with the lemon juice and zest. Heat a large skillet over medium heat and add half the dressing, followed by the chicken breasts. Cook until browned and add the vegetables.
3. Stir in remaining dressing and cook for 5 minutes.
4. Serve the chicken with the noodles.

Best Ever Roasted Chicken
Serves 4-6

Ingredients:

1 3-4 pound whole chicken
1 8-ounce bottle Italian dressing
1 pound baby carrots
4 stalks celery, cut into chunks

Directions:

1. Preheat oven to 350 degrees F.
2. Carefully separate the skin from the meat of the chicken. Brush the bottom with a quarter of the dressing. Tuck the wings under the breast and put the chicken on a roasting pan, breast side up.
3. Brush 1/2 cup of the dressing under the skin and all around the outside of the chicken.
4. Combine the carrots and celery in a bowl with the remaining 1/4 cup of dressing. Add to the roasting pan around the chicken.
5. Roast for 2 hours, or until chicken reaches 165 degrees. Allow to rest for 10 minutes before serving.
6. Serve the chicken with the vegetables.

Greek Roasted Chicken
Serves 4-6

Ingredients:

1 3-4 pound whole chicken
1 lemon
1/2 cup Greek dressing

Directions:

1. Preheat oven to 350 degrees F.
2. Cut the lemon in half and squeeze the juice into a small bowl. Put the juiced pieces inside the chicken cavity.
3. Ad the juice to the dressing and brush over the chicken.
4. Bake for 2 hours, or until chicken reaches 165 degrees. Allow to rest for 10 minutes before serving.

Pineapple Chicken and Ham
Serves 4

Ingredients:

4 boneless, skinless chicken breasts
1/2 cup balsamic vinaigrette dressing
1 can pineapple slices
4 slices honey ham
4 slices mozzarella cheese

Directions:

1. Preheat oven to 350 degrees F.
2. Lay the chicken breasts in a baking dish. Brush with the balsamic vinaigrette dressing.
3. Lay 1-2 pineapple slices on each chicken breast, followed by a slice of ham, and a slice of cheese.
4. Cover and bake for 30-40 minutes, until chicken is cooked through.

Soups and Stews

What's better on a chilly fall or cold winter night than a big bowl of soup? Soup warms the soul, but the thought of prepping the ingredients and simmering all day can be daunting.

Luckily, with the recipes in this section, you don't have to do that. Here you'll find a variety of soups that make for a hearty meal any time you have a craving. Creamy potato, cheesy broccoli, or spicy black bean are only some of the options you have when it comes to soups that come together in minutes and are ready to eat when you are. Best of all, you can make them in one pot, so there's virtually no clean up!

The next time you're looking for a great soup that comes together fast, look no further than these dump recipes the whole family will love. After one bite, you'll wonder why anyone slaves away in the kitchen for a pot of soup!

Chicken Tortilla Soup

Serves 4

Ingredients:

1 15-ounce can black beans, undrained
1 15-ounce can chicken broth (MS2)
1 15-ounce can Rotel tomatoes, undrained
1 15-ounce can corn, undrained
2 cups shredded or chopped cooked chicken
Garnishes: Shredded cheese, tortilla chips, sour cream

Directions:

1. Dump beans, broth and tomatoes in a soup pot. Add the chicken.
2. Bring to a boil. Reduce heat.
3. Serve hot, topped with desired garnishes.

Italian Ranch Chicken Soup
Serves 4

Ingredients:

1 teaspoon vegetable oil
2 cups chopped chicken breast
1 15-ounce can green beans, undrained
1 15-ounce can chicken broth (MS2)
1 15-ounce can white beans of your choice, undrained
1 15-ounce can diced tomatoes, undrained
1 10-ounce package frozen spinach, broken up
1 packet Ranch dressing mix (MS6)

Directions:

1. Heat a teaspoon oil to a large pot. Add the chicken and cook.
2. Add remaining ingredients to the pot.
3. Bring to a boil. Reduce heat to a simmer. Simmer until chicken is cooked through and soup is hot.
4. Serve hot with crusty bread, if desired.

Cheesy Broccoli Soup
Serves 2-4

Ingredients:

1 10-ounce package frozen, chopped broccoli
1 10-ounce can cream of chicken soup
1 1/2 cups milk
8 ounces Velveeta cheese, cubed

Directions:

1. Steam the broccoli according the directions on the package. Transfer to a soup pot.
2. Add the cream of chicken soup and one cup milk to the pan. Stir and heat over medium low heat.
3. Add the cheese and stir until melted. Add more milk to thin if desired.
4. Serve hot.

Italian White Bean Soup

Serves 4

Ingredients:

1 15-ounce can chicken stock (MS2)
2 15-ounce cans white beans, undrained
1 tablespoon Italian seasoning
1 15-ounce can diced tomatoes, undrained
1 10-ounce package frozen spinach, broken up

Directions:

1. Add the chicken stock, beans, seasoning and tomatoes to a soup pot.
2. Bring to a boil. Reduce heat and simmer.
3. About 5 minutes before serving, add the spinach and simmer until heated through.
4. Serve hot, with crusty bread if desired.

Tip: For a creamy version of this soup, puree half of the beans in a blender before adding them. This lends a silkiness to this soup, yet keeps it healthy!

Easy Hamburger Soup
Serves 6-8

Ingredients:

1 pound 90 % ground beef
3 cups water
1 15-ounce can green beans, undrained
1 15-ounce can corn, undrained
1 28-ounce can diced tomatoes
1 15-ounce can tomato sauce
2 cups macaroni or similar pasta
1/2 teaspoon Lawry's Seasoned Salt
1/2 teaspoon Mrs. Dash

Directions:

1. Heat a large pot over medium heat and add the ground beef and water. Break it up with a spatula and cook until it's no longer pink.
2. Add the remaining ingredients to the pot and bring to a boil. Reduce heat and simmer until pasta is done.
3. Serve hot.

Easy Bean and Bacon Soup
Serves 4

Ingredients:

1 15-ounce can Ranch beans
1 8-ounce can tomato sauce
1 15-ounce can chicken broth (MS2)
1/2 small onion, chopped
5-6 slices bacon, cooked and crumbled
1 teaspoon Morton's Nature Seasoning

Directions:

1. Combine all ingredients except bacon in a saucepan or soup pot.
2. Bring to a boil. Reduce heat to a simmer. Simmer for 15 minutes.
3. Add bacon and serve hot.

Tip: If you would like make the soup thicker, use a potato masher to mash up some of the beans. This will make it creamier, and slightly thicker.

Extra Tip: If you prefer, start with raw bacon, brown with onion, remove some of the fat with tongs and a wadded paper towel, and then add remaining ingredients.

Chicken and Wild Rice Soup
Serves 6-8

Ingredients:

1/2 cup butter
3/4 cup flour
2 5-ounce cans evaporated milk
2 15-ounce cans chicken stock (MS2)
2 cups water
2 cups chopped or shredded cooked chicken (TS2)
1 package instant long grain wild rice
1 teaspoon Lawry's Seasoned Salt

Directions:

1. Add the butter to a large soup pot. Heat on medium low heat. When melted stir in the flour. Stir until smooth.
2. Add the cream and stir until well combined. Add the stock, water, chicken, rice, and seasoning.
3. Cover and cook for 15 minutes, until rice is cooked through.
4. Serve hot.

Quick and Easy Beef Stew
Serves 4

Ingredients:

1 tablespoon butter or vegetable oil
1 pound boneless sirloin, cut into bite sized pieces
1 can condensed tomato soup or tomato sauce
1 can cream of mushroom soup
1 package Lipton Onion Soup (MS3)
1 24 ounce bag frozen stew vegetables (or make a mix of your favorite frozen veggies, totaling about 5 cups)
1 teaspoon Lawry's Seasoned Salt

Directions:

1. Heat the oil in large pot. Add the beef and cook until browned.
2. Add the soups and the vegetables, and the seasoning. Bring to a boil. Cover and reduce heat.
3. Simmer over low heat for 10-15 minutes until sauce is thickened and veggies are tender.
4. Serve hot.

Spicy Black Bean Soup
Serves 6

Ingredients:

3 15-ounce cans black beans, drained
1 15-ounce can Rotel tomatoes, drained
2 15-ounce cans chicken broth
1 teaspoon taco seasoning (MS1)
Sour cream, for serving

Directions:

1. Put 2 cans of beans, Rotel tomatoes, and 1 cup chicken broth in a blender. Blend until smooth.
2. Add the last can of beans to a large saucepan. Pour blended mixture over and bring to a simmer.
3. Serve the soup hot, with rice if desired. Top with sour cream.

Easy Pumpkin Soup
Serves 4

Ingredients:

1 can condensed cream of potato soup
1 cup water
1 15-ounce can pumpkin puree (make sure it's not pie filling!)
1 cup cream or half and half (MS4)
2 tablespoons butter
1/2 teaspoon garlic powder

Directions:

1. Combine all ingredients in a large saucepan over medium heat. Stir.
2. Simmer for 10-15 minutes.
3. Serve hot.

Tip: This is a favorite of mine to serve for company, and it also makes a nice Thanksgiving appetizer.

Super Easy Minestrone
Serves 4

Ingredients:

2 15-ounce cans chicken broth (MS2)
1 15-ounce can chickpeas or white beans, drained
1 15-ounce can diced tomatoes, undrained
1 bag Italian style frozen vegetables
1/2 cup fusilli pasta or elbow macaroni, uncooked
1/4 cup prepared Italian dressing
Grated Parmesan cheese, for serving

Directions:

1. Combine all ingredients except for the cheese in a large saucepan. Bring to a boil.
2. Reduce heat and simmer for 8-10 minutes, until pasta is tender.
3. Serve hot, topped with the Parmesan cheese.

Deeply D'Lish
Pizza - Page 29

Beef and Broccoli
Stir Fry - Page 36

Meatball Casserole - Page 47

Meatloaf and Mashed Potato Muffins - Page 88

Mexican Pizza - Page 91

Asian Lettuce Wraps - Page 95

Quick and Easy Steak Fajitas - Page 98

Roasted Chicken and Vegetable
Dinner - Page 108

Chicken with Creamy
Bacon Sauce - Page 127

Cheesy Broccoli Soup - Page 136

Game Day Chili - Page 148

Caramel Pull Apart Bread - Page 174

Lemon Pepper Roasted
Asparagus - Page 189

Super Easy Cheesy Bread Sticks - Page 216

Open Face Fajita Omelet - Page 230

Coconut Chicken Stew - Page 231

Cheesy Potato Soup
Serves 6

Ingredients:

1 can cream of chicken soup
1/2 package cream cheese
4 cups milk
1 16-ounce package frozen hash brown potatoes
1 tablespoon butter
1 teaspoon Morton's Nature Seasoning
2 cups shredded cheddar cheese
Garnishes: green onions, bacon bits, sour cream

Directions:

1. Add chicken soup and cream cheese to a large soup pot.
2. Whisk in the milk, a little at a time, until smooth and creamy.
3. Add the potatoes, butter, and seasoning and stir.
4. Bring to a boil, then reduce heat to a simmer. Simmer until potatoes are tender, about 20-30 minutes. Stir in cheese.
5. Serve hot.

Italian Style Tortellini Soup
Serves 4

Ingredients:

3 15-ounce cans chicken broth
1 15-ounce can Italian style stewed tomatoes
1 16-ounce package frozen tortellini, any style
1 10-ounce package frozen spinach, chopped
1 teaspoon Mrs. Dash

Directions:

1. Bring chicken broth to a boil. Add the tortellini and cook for about 6 minutes.
2. In the same pot, add the rest of the ingredients. Stir and simmer for 10 minutes.
3. Serve hot, with crusty bread if desired.

Mushroom and Wild Rice Soup
Serves 6-8

Ingredients:

1/2 cup butter
3/4 cup flour
2 cans evaporated milk
2 15-ounce cans chicken stock (MS2)
2 cups water
2 small cans mushrooms, drained
1 6-ounce package instant long grain wild rice
1 teaspoon Morton's Nature Seasoning

Directions:

1. Add the butter to a large soup pot. Heat on medium low heat. When melted stir in the flour. Stir until smooth.
2. Add the cream and stir until well combined. Add the stock, water, mushrooms and rice.
3. Cover and cook for 15 minutes, until rice is cooked through.
4. Serve hot.

Game Day Chili
Serves 4

Ingredients:

1 pound cooked ground beef (TS1)
2 15-ounce cans pinto beans, undrained
2 15-ounce cans Rotel tomatoes, undrained
1 onion, minced
2 tablespoons chili powder
Toppings of your choice: diced onion, shredded cheese, sour cream, chives, etc.

Directions:

1. Combine all ingredients in a large soup pot.
2. Bring to a boil. Reduce heat and simmer for 20-25 minutes until thickened.

Cure a Cold Chicken Noodle Soup
Serves 4

Ingredients:

1 tablespoon butter
2 cups chopped chicken
1 onion, chopped
2 ribs celery, chopped
2 carrots, chopped
2 15-ounce cans chicken broth (MS2)
4 cups water
2 cups egg noodles, uncooked
1 teaspoon Italian seasoning

Directions:

1. Heat the butter in a large soup pot. Add the chicken, onions, celery and carrots.
2. Cook until tender, about 10 minutes.
3. Add chicken broth, noodles, and seasoning.
4. Bring to a boil. Reduce heat and simmer for 20 minutes.
5. Serve hot.

Home Style Vegetable Soup
Serves 4

Ingredients:

1 15-ounce can chicken broth (MS2)
1 cup water
1 large potato, peeled and diced
1 15-ounce can diced tomatoes, undrained
1 15-ounce can green beans, undrained
1 15-ounce can corn kernels, undrained
1 teaspoon seasoned salt

Directions:

1. Combine all ingredients in a large soup pot.
2. Bring to a boil. Reduce to a simmer.
3. Simmer for 10-15 minutes.
4. Serve hot.

Tip: If you have leftover veggies or meat, this is a great recipe to use them up.

Shrimp and Corn Chowder
Serves 4

Ingredients:

1 can condensed potato soup
1 1/2 cups whole milk
1 15-ounce can corn, drained
1/2 pound peeled and deveined cooked shrimp
1/4 cup chopped fresh chives
1 teaspoon Morton's Nature Seasoning

Directions:

1. Combine the soup, milk and corn in a large saucepan. Bring to a boil and reduce heat.
2. Simmer for 10 minutes.
3. Add the shrimp, chives, and seasoning, and simmer for 5 more minutes.
4. Serve hot.

Southwest White Bean Soup

Serves 4

Ingredients:

1 15-ounce can chicken broth (MS2)
1 jar prepared picante sauce
1 15-ounce can white beans, drained
1 15-ounce can corn kernels, drained
2 cups shredded or chopped cooked chicken (TS2)
Garnishes: shredded cheese, sour cream, or broken tortilla chips

Directions:

1. Combine all ingredients in a large soup pot. Bring to a boil. Reduce heat.
2. Simmer for 10 minutes, until hot and bubbly.
3. Serve hot, topped with desired garnishes

Turkey and Corn Chowder

Serves 4

Ingredients:

1 can condensed cream of potato soup
1 1/2 cups milk
1/2 cup prepared salsa
1 8-ounce can corn, drained
2 cups cooked and cubed turkey (TS2)
5-6 slices bacon, cooked and crumbled (TS6)

Directions:

1. Combine all ingredients in a soup pot over medium high heat.
2. Bring to a boil. Reduce to a simmer and cook for 10 minutes.
3. Serve hot.

Quick Breakfast and Brunch Dishes

Breakfast is the most important meal of the day, but for most of us, it's also the busiest. That means we don't eat, or we grab a doughnut on the way to work.

Well, I think this is unacceptable, which is why this section is full of recipes that are filling, easy to make, and delicious. Whether you're looking for something to get your weekday off to the right start, or something for a lazy Sunday brunch, you'll find it here.

Easy Cheesy Breakfast Bake
Serves 4-6

Ingredients:

1 tube Grands biscuits, separated and cut in quarters.
1 cup egg beaters or 3 eggs beaten with 1/4 cup milk.
1 cup precooked sausage crumbles or 8 slices
precooked bacon, cut into 1" pieces.
3/4 cup shredded cheese

Directions:

1. Preheat oven to 350.
2. Spray 9 x 13 pan with nonstick spray.
3. Arrange biscuit pieces in single layer in pan.
4. Distribute bacon or sausage evenly over biscuits.
5. Pour egg over all.
6. Sprinkle evenly with cheese.
7. Bake for 20 to 25 minutes, until egg is set and biscuits are brown.

Mexican Breakfast Pie
Serves 8

Ingredients:

1 pre rolled piecrust
6 eggs
12/ cup milk
1 can Rotel tomatoes, drained
1 teaspoon taco seasoning (MS1)
1/2 cup black olives
1 cup shredded Mexican cheese

Directions:

1. Preheat oven to 400 degrees F. Lay the pie crust in a pie plate and crimp the edges, cutting off excess.
2. Be a the eggs with the milk. Add the tomatoes, taco seasoning, and olives and pour the mixture into the pie crust. Sprinkle with cheese.
3. Bake for 20-25 minutes, until eggs are set and cheese is lightly browned.

Cinnamon Roll Donuts
Serves 8

Ingredients:

1 can cinnamon rolls (My favorite are the Pillsbury Cinnabon ones)
Vegetable oil, for frying

Directions:

1. If you have a deep fryer, fill it with oil and preheat. If not, fill a shallow pot or pan with about 2 inches of vegetable oil and heat.
2. Open the can of cinnamon rolls. Push thumb through the center and form donut shape or cut out center and fry for donut holes.
3. When your oil is hot, carefully add the cinnamon rolls. Don't walk away!
4. When golden brown, flip and cook the other side until golden brown.
5. Drain on paper towels and drizzle with icing or sprinkle with powdered sugar. These are best served warm!

Dijon Chicken Quiche
Serves 6-8

Ingredients:

1 pre rolled piecrust
6 eggs
1 tablespoon Dijon mustard
1 can condensed cream of mushroom soup
1/2 cup milk
1 cup chopped or shredded cooked chicken (TS2)
1/2 cup grated Parmesan cheese

Directions:

1. Preheat oven to 400 degrees F. Lay the pie crust in a pie plate and crimp the edges, cutting off excess.
2. Beat the eggs with the mustard. Stir in the soup and milk. Add the chicken and pour the mixture into the prepared pie crust. Sprinkle the cheese on top.
3. Bake for 25-30 minutes until eggs are set and cheese is browned.

Amazing Apple Coffee Cake

Serves 6

Ingredients:

2 cups baking mix, such as Bisquick
2/3 cup milk
2 tablespoons sugar
1/2 teaspoon cinnamon
1 egg
1 apple, cored, peeled and chopped

Directions:

1. Preheat oven to 400 degrees F. Lightly spray an 8 inch cake pan with cooking spray.
2. Combine all of the ingredients in a large bowl and then pour into prepared pan.
3. Bake for 20 minutes, until a toothpick inserted in the center comes out clean.

Blender Waffles
Serves 10-12

Ingredients:

1 1/3 cup milk
1 large egg
2 tablespoons vegetable oil or melted butter
2 cups prepared baking mix, such as Bisquick

Directions:

1. Preheat your waffle iron.
2. Put the eggs, milk, and oil in your blender. Blend on medium speed until well combined.
3. Add the baking mix and pulse or blend on low until just combined.
4. Spray your waffle iron with cooking spray, and fill evenly with batter, according to your manufacturers instructions. Cook until golden browned.
5. Serve with warm syrup and butter.

Italian Skillet Frittata
Serves 4

Ingredients:

8 eggs
1/4 cup milk
2 tablespoons butter or vegetable oil
1/4 cup diced ham
1/4 cup chopped olives
1 cup chopped spinach
1/4 cup grated Parmesan cheese

Directions:

1. Preheat oven to 350 degrees F.
2. Beat the eggs with the milk. Heat a large, ovenproof skillet over medium heat. Add the butter, followed by the eggs.
3. Add the ham, olives and spinach and stir carefully. Transfer the skillet to the oven and bake for 10-15 minutes, until eggs are set.
4. Remove from the oven, sprinkle with cheese, and serve.

Fiesta Scramble
Serves 4

Ingredients:

8 large eggs
1/4 cup milk
1 tablespoon butter
1/4 cup cooked and crumbled bacon (TS6)
1/2 can Rotel tomatoes
1/2 cup shredded cheese

Directions:

1. Beat the eggs with the milk. Heat a large, non-stick skillet over medium heat and add the butter.
2. Pour the egg mixture in the skillet and stir in the bacon and tomatoes. With a rubber spatula, stir the eggs until they are cooked through.
3. When eggs are cooked, sprinkle cheese evenly over top and serve.

Tip: I like to serve this topped with a dollop of sour cream and a sprinkle of green onions. It's also delicious when topped with your favorite salsa.

Bacon and Sausage Scramble
Serves 4

Ingredients:

8 large eggs
1/4 cup milk
1 tablespoon butter
1/4 cup cooked and crumbled bacon (TS6)
1/4 cup cooked and crumbled breakfast sausage
1/2 cup shredded cheese

Directions:

1. Beat the eggs with the milk. Heat a large, non-stick skillet over medium heat and add the butter.
2. Pour the egg mixture in the skillet and stir in the bacon and sausage. With a rubber spatula, stir the eggs until they are cooked through.
3. When eggs are cooked, sprinkle cheese evenly over top and serve.

Breakfast Pull Apart Bread
Serves 8

Ingredients:

1 can refrigerated biscuits
1 tablespoon milk
1 egg
1/2 cup shredded cheddar cheese
1/4 cup cooked and crumbled bacon (TS6)
1/4 cup cooked and crumbled sausage

Directions:

1. Preheat oven to 350 degrees F. Spray a large casserole dish with cooking spray.
2. Cut the biscuits into 3 or 4 pieces each and lay them in a large casserole dish.
3. Beat the eggs with the milk. Toss the bacon, sausage and cheese with the biscuits and pour over the egg mixture. Stir until everything is evenly coated.
4. Bake for 20-25 minutes, until biscuits are golden brown. Serve warm.

Chicken Broccoli and Cheese Quiche
Serves 6-8

Ingredients:

1 pre rolled piecrust
6 eggs
1/2 cup milk
1 bag frozen chopped broccoli florets
1 can condensed cream of mushroom soup
1 cup chopped or shredded cooked chicken (TS2)
1/2 cup shredded cheddar cheese

Directions:

1. Preheat oven to 400 degrees F. Lay the pie crust in a pie plate and crimp the edges, cutting off excess.
2. Beat the eggs with the milk. Stir in the broccoli, soup, and chicken, and pour the mixture into the prepared pie crust. Sprinkle the cheese on top.
3. Bake for 25-30 minutes until eggs are set and cheese is browned.

Creamy Three Cheese Quiche
Serves 6-8

Ingredients:

1 pre rolled piecrust
6 eggs
1/2 cup milk
1 can condensed cheddar cheese soup
1/2 cup shredded cheddar cheese
1/2 cup grated Parmesan cheese

Directions:

1. Preheat oven to 400 degrees F. Lay the pie crust in a pie plate and crimp the edges, cutting off excess.
2. Beat the eggs with the milk. Stir in the soup and pour the mixture into the prepared pie crust. Sprinkle the remaining cheese on top.
3. Bake for 25-30 minutes until eggs are set and cheese is browned.

Taco Quiche

Serves 8

Ingredients:

1 pre rolled piecrust
6 eggs
12/ cup milk
1 can Rotel tomatoes, drained
1 can corn kernels, drained
1 teaspoon taco seasoning (MS1)
1 cup shredded Mexican cheese
1/4 cup chopped green onions

Directions:

1. Preheat oven to 400 degrees F. Lay the pie crust in a pie plate and crimp the edges, cutting off excess.
2. Be a the eggs with the milk. Add the tomatoes, corn, and taco seasoning and pour the mixture into the pie crust. Sprinkle with cheese.
3. Bake for 20-25 minutes, until eggs are set and cheese is lightly browned.
4. Top with the green onions before serving.

Breakfast Meat Scramble
Serves 6

Ingredients:

12 eggs
1/4 cup milk
2 tablespoons butter
6 slices bacon, cooked and crumbled (TS6)
4 sausage links, cooked and diced
4 slices ham, chopped

Directions:

1. Beat the eggs with the milk. Heat a large non stick skillet over medium heat and add the butter. Pour in the eggs, followed by the bacon, sausage, and ham.
2. Stir with a rubber spatula, scrambling the eggs until they are cooked through and serve.

Veggie Brunch Bake
Serves 6

Ingredients:

12 eggs
1/4 cup milk
1 bag frozen mixed vegetables of your choice
1 can condensed cream of mushroom soup
3 cups fresh chopped spinach
1/2 cup grated Parmesan cheese

Directions:

1. Preheat oven to 350 degrees F. Lightly spray a 2 quart casserole dish with cooking spray.
2. Beat the eggs with the milk. Stir in the vegetables, soup, and chopped spinach.
3. Pour into prepared dish and bake for 20-25 minutes, until eggs are set. Sprinkle the cheese on top before serving.

Breakfast Bread Pudding
Serves 8

Ingredients:

8 slices cinnamon bread, cubed
8 eggs
2 cups milk
1 teaspoon ground cinnamon
1 tablespoon maple syrup

Directions:

1. Preheat oven to 350 degrees F. Lightly spray a 3 quart baking dish with cooking spray.
2. Lay the bread cubes in an even layer in the dish. Beat the eggs with the milk, cinnamon, and maple syrup. Pour over the bread.
3. Bake for 45 minutes, until top is golden brown. Serve with additional maple syrup.

Bacon and Hash Brown Casserole
Serves 8

Ingredients:

1 16 ounce bag frozen hash browns, thawed
10 slices bacon, cut into bite sized pieces
1/2 cup chopped onion (TS3)
8 eggs
1/2 cup milk
1 cup shredded cheddar cheese

Directions:

1. Preheat oven to 350 degrees F. Spray a large casserole dish with cooking spray. Lay the potatoes in the dish.
2. Heat a large skillet over medium heat and add the bacon and onions. Cook until bacon is crisp.
3. Beat the eggs with the milk and add the bacon and onion mixture. Pour over the hash browns. Cover and bake for 40 minutes, until eggs are set.
4. Remove from oven and top with the cheese. Pop back in the oven for 5-10 minutes until cheese is melted and bubbly.

Overnight Oven French Toast
Serves 4

Ingredients:

8 thick slices bread
6 eggs
2 cups milk
1/4 cup sugar
1 teaspoon vanilla

Directions:

1. Spray a large baking dish with cooking spray.
2. Lay the bread slices in the dish.
3. Beat the eggs with the milk, sugar, and vanilla. Pour over the bread. Cover and refrigerate overnight.
4. In the morning, preheat oven to 400 degrees F. Uncover dish and bake for 25-30 minutes until top is browned.

Tip: This is my favorite breakfast for company since you do minimal work the night before and just pop it in the oven when you're ready to eat. It's delicious, easy, and everyone, including the kids, absolutely loves it!

Easy Breakfast Pizza
Serves 4

Ingredients:

1 teaspoon oil
6 eggs
1/4 cup milk
1 large ready to heat pizza crust
1/2 cup shredded cheddar cheese
4 slices bacon, cooked and crumbled (TS6)

Directions:

1. Preheat oven to 350 degrees F. Lay the pizza crust on a baking sheet.
2. Heat the oil in a large non stick skillet. Beat the eggs with the milk and pour in the pan. Scramble the eggs until cooked through and then lay evenly on the pizza crust.
3. Top with cheese and bake for 8 minutes, until cheese is melted.
4. Top with bacon, slice, and serve.

Caramel Pull Apart Bread
Serves 12

Ingredients:

2 cans refrigerated biscuits
1 cup brown sugar
1 small can evaporated milk
1 teaspoon ground cinnamon

Directions:

1. Preheat oven to 350 degrees F. Spray a Bundt pan with cooking spray.
2. Cut the biscuits into quarters and layer in pan.
3. Combine the brown sugar with the evaporated milk and cinnamon. Pour over biscuits.
4. Bake for 30-40 minutes, until biscuits are browned. Remove from oven and let sit for 10 minutes before turning over onto a plate. These are best served warm!

Breakfast Enchiladas

Serves:

Ingredients:

1/2 pound ground beef (TS1)
4 eggs, lightly beaten
1 jar your favorite salsa
2 cups shredded Mexican style cheese
12 flour tortillas

Directions:

1. Preheat oven to 350 degrees F.
2. Heat a skillet over medium heat and add the beef. When cooked through, stir in the eggs and stir until cooked. Stir in half the salsa and half the cheese. Stir until heated and cheese is melted.
3. Pour half of the remaining salsa in the bottom of a large casserole dish.
4. Spoon some of the beef and egg filling down the center of each tortilla and lay seam side down in the casserole dish. When all tortillas are filled, top with remaining salsa and cheese.
5. Bake for 15-20 minutes, until cheese is melted.

Easy Side Dishes For Every Meal

Looking for an easy side for a weeknight meal or to take to a potluck? You'll find them in this section. Whether you're looking for something super healthy like spinach, or more comforting like potatoes, it's here.

These sides are easy and fast, and can come together in the last few minutes of cooking. With little prep work, they're tasty, quick, and involve minimal cleanup. Best of all, the whole family will love them.

Mushroom Rice Pilaf
Serves 4

Ingredients:

1 tablespoon butter
1/2 cup chopped onion (TS3)
1 small can sliced mushrooms, drained
1 cup white rice
2 cups chicken stock (TS4)

Directions:

1. Heat a medium saucepan over medium heat. Add the butter, onions and mushrooms, and cook for 5 minutes.
2. Add the rice, stir, and add the stock. Bring to a boil. Reduce heat to a simmer.
3. Cover and cook for 20 minutes over low heat. Fluff with a fork before serving.

Easy Squash and Corn Sauté
Serves 4

Ingredients:

1 teaspoon butter or vegetable oil
1 small zucchini, diced
1 small yellow squash, diced
1 can corn kernels, drained
1/2 packet Italian dressing seasoning (MS8)

Directions:

1. Heat a skillet over medium heat and add the butter. Add the zucchini and squash and cook for 5 minutes, until tender. Stir in the corn and cook until heated through.
2. Stir in the seasoning and stir well. Serve.

Green Bean Casserole with a Kick

Serves 4-6

Ingredients:

1 can condensed cream of mushroom soup
1/2 cup milk
1 teaspoon hot sauce
2 cans green beans, drained
1 cup French fried onions

Directions:

1. Preheat oven to 350 degrees F.
2. Combine the soup, milk, hot sauce, green beans, and half the onions in a 2-quart casserole dish.
3. Bake for 30 minutes until the casserole is bubbly. Top with the remaining fried onions and serve.

Vegetable and Bacon Sauté
Serves 4

Ingredients:

2 strips bacon, chopped
1 bag frozen mixed vegetables (Our family loves corn, peas, and carrots, but anything will do!)
1/2 packet Lipton onion soup (MS3)

Directions:

1. Heat a large skillet over medium heat and add the bacon. Cook until crisp and add the vegetables and onion soup. Stir and continue cooking until veggies are heated through and serve.

Honey Mustard Roasted Potatoes

Serves 4

Ingredients:

1 pound small red potatoes, halved
1/4 cup chopped onion (TS3)
1/4 cup Honey mustard salad dressing

Directions:

2. Preheat oven to 400 degrees F. Spray a baking sheet with cooking spray.
3. Toss the potatoes with the onion and dressing and spread in an even layer on the baking sheet.
4. Bake for 35-40 minutes, until potatoes are tender when pierced with a fork.

Creamy Cabbage and Bacon

Serves 4-6

Ingredients:

4 slices bacon, chopped
4 cups shredded cabbage
1 can condensed cream of mushroom soup
1/2 cup milk

Directions:

1. Heat a large skillet over medium heat. Add the bacon and cook until almost crisp. Add the cabbage and continue cooking until soft, about 8 minutes.
2. Add the soup and the milk and stir. Bring to a boil and reduce heat. Simmer until cabbage is soft.

Super Fast Sautéed Spinach
Serves 4

Ingredients:

2 slices bacon, chopped
1/2 cup chopped onion (TS3)
1/2 teaspoon garlic powder
1 12-ounce bag baby spinach

Directions:

1. Heat a large skillet over medium heat. Add the bacon, onion, and garlic powder and cook until the bacon is crisp.
2. Add the spinach to the pan, getting all of it into the pan as quickly as possible. Stir and cook until spinach is wilted, about 3 minutes. Serve.

Tip: When served with baked chicken, this is one of my family's favorite meals. It comes together super fast, and even spinach haters seem to eat this right up!

Italian Roasted Veggies
Serves 4

Ingredients:

1 tablespoon vegetable oil
1 bag frozen broccoli florets
1 bag bell pepper and onion mix (the kind you might use for stir fry)
1/2 packet Italian dressing seasoning mix (MS8)

Directions:

1. Preheat oven to 400 degrees F. Lightly spray a baking sheet with cooking spray.
2. Toss the vegetables with the oil and seasoning. Lay in a single layer on the baking sheet.
3. Roast for 30-35 minutes, until veggies are soft and lightly charred.

Creamy Cheesy Cauliflower
Serves 4

Ingredients:

1 bag frozen cauliflower florets
1 can condensed cream of mushroom soup
1/2 cup milk
4 ounces Velveeta, cubed

Directions:

1. Combine the cauliflower, mushroom soup, and milk in a medium saucepan. Heat until creamy and smooth and allow to simmer for 8-10 minutes, until cauliflower is tender.
2. Stir in the Velveeta until melted.

Skillet Corn and Peppers
Serves 4

Ingredients:

4 slices bacon, chopped
1/2 cup chopped onion (TS3)
1/2 cup chopped bell peppers
1 can corn kernels, drained
1 teaspoon taco seasoning (MS1)

Directions:

1. Heat a large skillet over medium heat. Add the bacon, onions, and peppers. Cook until bacon is crisp and veggies are soft. Add the corn and taco seasoning and continue cooking until heated through.

Tip: This is delicious served with enchiladas, or my Fiesta Style Chicken (found in section 6 of this book). You can also used it as an addition to taco filling, or as a side dish for any chicken dish.

Roasted Root Vegetables
Serves 4

Ingredients:

1 tablespoon vegetable oil
1 large potato, peeled and cubed
1 large carrot, peeled and sliced
1 large turnip, peeled and cubed
1/2 packet Italian dressing seasoning mix (MS8)

Directions:

1. Preheat oven to 400 degrees F. Spray a large baking sheet with cooking spray.
2. Toss the vegetables with the oil and seasoning. Lay on the baking sheet in a single layer.
3. Roast for 35-40 minutes, until vegetables are tender and lightly caramelized.

Tip: You can easily customize this using whatever root veggies you have on hand. My family has enjoyed various combinations of beets, sweet potatoes, and parsnips along with the veggies listed above. They make an easy and delicious side dish to winter roasts.

Easiest Bacon BBQ Beans
Serves 4

Ingredients:

1/2 cup chopped onion (TS3)
4 slices bacon, chopped
2 cans baked beans
1 tablespoon mustard
1 tablespoon brown sugar
1 tablespoon molasses

Directions:

Preheat oven to 350 degrees F.
Cook the onion and bacon in a medium skillet until onions are soft, being careful not to let the bacon get too crispy.
Transfer to a 2-quart casserole dish and stir in the remaining ingredients.
Cover and bake for 1 hour.

Lemon Pepper Roasted Asparagus
Serves 4

Ingredients:

1 large bunch asparagus
1 tablespoon vegetable oil
1 teaspoon lemon pepper seasoning

Directions:

1. Preheat oven to 400 degrees F. Spray a large baking sheet with cooking spray.
2. Toss the asparagus with the oil and seasoning.
3. Roast for 10-12 minutes, until asparagus is tender.

Crunchy Cracker Stuffing
Serves 8

Ingredients:

4 slices bacon, chopped
1/2 cup chopped onion (TS3)
1/2 cup chopped celery
1/2 stick butter, melted
1 1-pound box crackers (My family loves Ritz crackers in this, but Saltines work as well!)
1 tablespoon poultry seasoning
2 cups chicken stock (TS4)
2 eggs, lightly beaten

Directions:

1. Preheat oven to 325 degrees F.
2. Heat a skillet over medium heat and add the bacon, onion and celery. Cook until vegetables are soft and transfer to a large bowl. Stir in the remaining ingredients and transfer mixture to a 2-quart casserole dish.
3. Cover and bake for 40 minutes.

Roasted Broccoli and Cauliflower
Serves 4

Ingredients:

1 bag frozen broccoli florets
1 bag frozen cauliflower florets
1 tablespoon vegetable oil
1/2 packet Italian dressing seasoning.

Directions:

1. Preheat oven to 400 degrees F. Lightly spray a baking sheet with cooking spray.
2. Toss the vegetables with the oil and seasoning. Lay in a single layer on the baking sheet.
3. Roast for 20-25 minutes, until veggies are soft and lightly charred.

Mashed Potato Casserole with Crunchy Topping

Serves 6

Ingredients:

3 cups leftover mashed potatoes
1 cup sour cream
1/4 cup milk
1/2 teaspoon garlic powder
1 cup corn flakes
1 cup shredded cheddar cheese

Directions:

1. Preheat oven to 350 degrees F.
2. Combine the mashed potatoes with the sour cream and milk in a medium saucepan. Heat on medium heat until hot. Stir in the garlic powder.
3. Spread the mashed potatoes into a 2-quart casserole dish. Top with the cornflakes and cheddar.
4. Bake for 30 minutes, until top is browned and casserole is bubbly.

Cheesy Bacon Corn Casserole
Serves 8-10

Ingredients:

1 can corn kernels, drained
1 can cream style corn
1 cup sour cream
1 box corn muffin mix (I like Jiffy!)
1 egg
4 slices bacon, cooked and crumbled (TS6)
1 cup shredded cheddar cheese

Directions:

1. Preheat oven to 350 degrees F. Spray a large casserole or baking dish with cooking spray.
2. Combine all ingredients except the cheese in a large bowl. Mix well and pour into baking dish.
3. Bake for 20 minutes, remove from oven and top with cheese.
4. Bake 20 more minutes, until cheese is melted and bubbly.

Broccoli and Rice Bake
Serves 8

Ingredients:

1 stick butter
1 cup chopped onion (TS3)
1 bag frozen broccoli florets
1/4 cup milk
1 can condensed cheddar cheese soup
1 can condensed cream of mushroom soup
1 1/2 cups cooked rice (TS8)

Directions:

1. Preheat oven to 350 degrees F.
2. Add the butter to a large skillet or saucepan and add the onion. Cook over medium heat until onion is soft. Add the broccoli and cook until tender. Ad the remaining ingredients and stir.
3. Pour the mixture into a 2-quart baking dish and bake for 30 minutes.

Southwest Stovetop Black Beans
Serves 4-6

Ingredients:

2 slices bacon, chopped
1/4 cup chopped onion
1 can black beans, drained
1 can Rotel tomatoes
1 teaspoon taco seasoning (MS1)

Directions:

1. Heat a medium saucepan over medium heat. Add the bacon and onion and cook until bacon is crisp.
2. Add the black beans, tomatoes, and taco seasoning and bring to a boil. Reduce heat and simmer for 10 minutes before serving.

Easy Skillet Potatoes
Serves 4

Ingredients:

2 tablespoons vegetable oil
1/2 cup chopped onion
2 large potatoes, peeled and chopped into small cubes
1/2 packet Ranch dressing seasoning (MS6)

Directions:

1. Heat the oil in a large skillet. Add the onions and potatoes and cook until potatoes are browned. Stir in the Ranch seasoning.
2. Continue cooking until potatoes are tender.

Easy Appetizers

Entertaining doesn't have to be difficult with these quick and easy appetizers. In this section, you'll find a variety of hot and cold appetizers, including dips, bite sized favorites, and more.

These easy crowd pleasers are all made with easy to find ingredients, some of which you probably always have on hand. You can make them for your own gathering or prepare them to take to a party. Either way, they are sure to please.

The next time you have a holiday party or even unexpected guests, you'll be able to quickly get one (or more!) of these ready to go in no time. Your guests will be impressed, yet you won't be stressed and overwhelmed.

Creamy Pesto Dip
Serves 6-8

Ingredients:

1 8 ounce package cream cheese, softened
1 4 ounce container prepared pesto
Crackers, pita chips, or veggies for serving

Directions:

1. Beat the cream cheese and pesto with a hand mixer until fluffy and well combined.
2. Transfer to a bowl and serve with crackers, chips, or veggies.

Baked Artichoke Dip
Serves 12

Ingredients:

1 14-ounce can artichoke hearts, drained
1 cup mayonnaise
1 cup grated Parmesan cheese
1 teaspoon garlic powder
Pita bread or tortilla chips, for serving

Directions:

1. Preheat oven to 350 degrees F.
2. Combine all ingredients in a large bowl. Stir until combined.
3. Transfer to a casserole dish or pie plate and bake for 25 minutes until bubbly and browned.
4. Serve with pita or tortilla chips.

Mexican Layered Dip
Serves 8

Ingredients:

1 can refried beans
1 tablespoon taco seasoning (MS1)
1 cup sour cream
1 cup shredded cheddar cheese
1/4 cup sliced black olives
1 tomato, chopped
Tortilla chips, for serving

Directions:

1. Combine the beans with the taco seasoning and spread in a casserole dish or pie plate.
2. Layer the remaining ingredients in order.
3. Refrigerate until chilled and serve with tortilla chips.

Easy Onion Dip
Serves 12

Ingredients:

2 cups mayonnaise
1 cup shredded Italian cheese blend
1/2 block cream cheese, softened
1 cup chopped onion (TS3)
Crackers, bread, or veggies for serving

Directions:

1. Preheat oven to 375 degrees F.
2. Combine all ingredients in a mixing bowl.
3. Spread into a baking dish.
4. Bake for 30 minutes.
5. Serve hot with crackers, bread, or veggies.

Quick Pizza Dip
Serves 12

Ingredients:

1 block cream cheese, softened
1/2 cup pizza sauce
1/2 cup shredded mozzarella cheese
1/2 cup chopped pepperoni
Crackers, for serving

Directions:

1. Preheat oven to 350 degrees F.
2. Combine the cream cheese and pizza sauce in a bowl and spread in a casserole dish.
3. Top with cheese and pepperoni.
4. Bake for 20 minutes, until cheese is bubbly.
5. Serve with crackers.

Super Easy Cheese Ball
Serves 12

Ingredients:

1 block cream cheese, softened
1 cup shredded mozzarella cheese
1 packet Lipton Onion Soup Mix (MS3)
2 tablespoons sour cream
1/2 cup finely chopped pecans
Crackers, for serving

Directions:

1. Combine the cream cheese, mozzarella, onion soup, and sour cream in a mixing bowl.
2. Shape mixture into a ball or log.
3. Refrigerate for 2 hours until firm.
4. Roll in chopped nuts.
5. Serve with crackers.

Zesty Chicken Wings
Serves 8

Ingredients:

1 cup Italian dressing
1/2 cup barbecue sauce
2 pounds chicken wings or drummettes

Directions:

1. Preheat oven to 450 degrees F.
2. Combine the Italian dressing and barbecue sauce and pour over the wings to coat.
3. Lay them on a foil lined baking sheet and bake for 30-45 minutes, until wings are browned and cooked through.

Beef Enchilada Dip
Serves 12

Ingredients:

1 pound cooked ground beef (TS1)
1 can condensed cream of chicken soup
1 1/2 cups Velveeta cubes
1 can Rotel tomatoes, undrained
Tortilla chips, for serving

Directions:

1. Preheat oven to 350 degrees F.
2. Combine the cooked ground beef with the soup and 1 cup Velveeta cubes.
3. Spread mixture in a baking dish. Top with remaining cheese and tomatoes.
4. Bake for 25 minutes, until bubbly.
5. Serve with tortilla chips.

Easy Chips and Salsa
Serves 12

Ingredients:

2 cans Rotel tomatoes, drained
1 can black beans, drained
1 small can corn kernels, drained
1 teaspoon taco seasoning (MS1)
Tortilla chips, for serving

Directions:

1. Combine the tomatoes, beans, corn, and taco seasoning in a serving bowl.
2. Chill until ready to serve.
3. Serve with tortilla chips.

Quick Italian Dip

Serves 12

Ingredients:

1 cup mayonnaise
1 cup sour cream
1 packet dry Italian dressing mix (MS8)
1/2 cup finely chopped bell peppers
Crackers, vegetables, or bread, for serving

Directions:

1. Combine the mayo, sour cream, Italian dressing mix, and bell peppers in a large bowl.
2. Refrigerate until chilled.
3. Serve with crackers, vegetables, and bread.

Easy Antipasto Finger Sandwiches
Serves 12

Ingredients:

1 French baguette
1 block cream cheese, softened
1/4 cup prepared pesto
1/2 cup sun dried tomatoes
1/2 cup artichoke hearts
1/4 cup grated Parmesan cheese
2 cups baby spinach leaves

Directions:

1. Cut the baguette in half lengthwise. Remove the insides from both pieces.
2. Combine the cream cheese and pesto and spread on the inside of the bread.
3. Add the rest of the ingredients and close the baguette.
4. Wrap tightly with plastic wrap and refrigerate for 45 minutes.
5. Slice before serving.

Jalapeño Cheddar Dip
Serves 12

Ingredients:

1 block cream cheese, softened
1/2 teaspoon garlic powder
5 slices bacon, cooked and crumbled (TS6)
1 cup shredded cheddar cheese
1 small can jalapeño peppers
Tortilla chips, for serving

Directions:

1. Preheat oven to 350 degrees F.
2. Combine all of the ingredients in a large mixing bowl.
3. Spread in a casserole dish.
4. Bake 20 minutes, until bubbly.
5. Serve with tortilla chips.

Creamy Spinach and Bacon Dip
Serves 12

Ingredients:

1 package frozen chopped spinach, chopped and drained
1 pound Velveeta, cubed
1/2 block cream cheese, softened
1 can Rotel tomatoes
6 slices bacon, cooked and crumbled (TS6)
Crackers, for serving

Directions:

1. Combine all ingredients in a large microwavable bowl.
2. Microwave on high for 3 minutes. Stir.
3. Continue microwaving until cheese is melted.
4. Serve with crackers.

Creamed Shrimp Cocktail
Serves 12

Ingredients:

1 block cream cheese, softened
1 pound cocktail shrimp, chopped
3/4 cup cocktail sauce
1/4 cup grated Parmesan cheese
Crackers, for serving

Directions:

1. Spread the cream cheese on the bottom of a serving dish.
2. Combine the shrimp and cocktail sauce and pour on top of the cream cheese.
3. Top with the cheese.
4. Serve with crackers.

Greek Layered Dip
Serves 12

Ingredients:

1 8-ounce container hummus
1/2 cup crumbled feta cheese
1/2 can diced tomatoes, drained
1/4 cup diced cucumbers
1/4 cup sliced olives
Pita chips, for serving

Directions:

1. Spread the hummus in a pie plate or casserole dish.
2. Layer the remaining ingredients on top.
3. Serve with the pita chips.

Taco Cheese Ball
Serves 12

Ingredients:

1 block cream cheese, softened
1 cup shredded pepper jack cheese
1 cup shredded cheddar cheese
1 can Rotel tomatoes, drained
1 teaspoon taco seasoning (MS1)
12 tortilla chips, finely crushed
Crackers, for serving

Directions:

1. Beat the cream cheese with the other cheeses until well combined.
2. Stir in the tomatoes and taco seasoning.
3. Form into a ball and refrigerate for one hour.
4. Roll in the tortilla chips.
5. Serve with crackers.

Pumpkin Spice Dip
Serves 12

Ingredients:

1 block cream cheese, softened
2 cup powdered sugar
1 can pumpkin pie filling
1 teaspoon pumpkin pie spice
Sliced apples and shortbread cookies, for serving

Directions:

1. Beat the cream cheese and powdered sugar until smooth.
2. Stir in the pumpkin pie filling and spice. Beat until creamy.
3. Chill overnight.
4. Serve with apples and cookies.

Italian Cheese Pie
Serves 8

Ingredients:

1 refrigerated piecrust, such as one from Pillsbury
1/2 cup Italian bread crumbs
1/4 cup grated Parmesan cheese
1 block cream cheese, softened
1/2 can diced tomatoes, drained

Directions:

1. Preheat oven to 400 degrees F.
2. Lay pie crust on a baking sheet. Roll into a 12-inch round.
3. Combine bread crumbs, cheeses, and tomatoes in a medium bowl.
4. Spread the mixture over the pie crust, leaving about 3 inches. Carefully fold the edges over the filling.
5. Bake 25-30 minutes until crust is golden brown.
6. Cool and cut into wedges.

Super Easy Cheesy Bread Sticks
Serves 8

Ingredients:

1 can crescent roll dough
1 teaspoon garlic powder
1 cup shredded cheddar cheese

Directions:

1. Preheat oven to 350 degrees F.
2. Leave the crescent roll dough in tact.
3. Spread it on a casserole dish and press into the pan, pressing the perforations together.
4. Sprinkle with the garlic powder and top with the cheddar cheese.
5. Bake for 12-15 minutes, until cheese is melted and lightly browned.
6. Remove from oven and allow to cool completely.
7. Use a pizza cutter to cut into sticks.

Spinach and Feta Crescents
Serves 8

Ingredients:

1 teaspoon garlic powder
1/2 cup crumbled feta cheese
1/2 cup grated Parmesan
1 cup baby spinach, chopped
1 crescent roll dough

Directions:

1. Preheat oven to 350 degrees F.
2. Combine the garlic powder, feta, Parmesan, and spinach in a medium bowl.
3. Divide the crescent rolls into triangles and fill with two teaspoons of cheese mixture.
4. Roll up and lay on a lightly greased cookie sheet.
5. Bake for 12-15 minutes until lightly golden.
6. Cool and serve.

Sausage Bites
Serves 16

Ingredients:

1 pound ground sausage
1 block cream cheese
2 cans crescent roll dough

Directions:

1. Preheat oven to 375 degrees F.
2. Cook sausage in a sauté pan and drain. Add the cream cheese and stir until combined.
3. Lay one package of crescent rolls on a baking sheet, leaving it in tact. Spread the sausage mixture on the dough.
4. Unroll the second can and lay on top. Press the seams together.
5. Bake for 20-25 minutes, until top is browned.
6. Allow to cool slightly and cut into 16 squares.

Taco Tartlets
Serves 24

Ingredients:

1 can biscuit dough
1/2 pound cooked ground beef (TS1)
2 teaspoons taco seasoning (MS1)
1 cup shredded cheddar cheese

Directions:

1. Preheat oven to 400 degrees F.
2. Cut the biscuit dough into 24 pieces and fill a mini muffin pan with the pieces.
3. Using your fingers, press down the dough until you have a bowl like shape.
4. Combine the ground beef with the taco seasoning. Fill each tart with the mixture.
5. Top with the cheese and bake for 20 minutes, until cheese is bubbly.
6. Serve warm.

Cook Once, Eat Twice

One way to make cooking on busy nights is to plan to make meals that will do double duty, which means knowing how to use leftovers. The recipes in this section will show you how.

You'll see two recipes for each set; the first one makes enough to have leftovers for the second recipe. You may think that this means simply reheating leftovers, but while that's okay for some nights, I find it can get boring after awhile. Instead, the second recipe is completely different, yet super easy to prepare because the cooking is mostly done!

Slow Cooked Pot Roast Turns into Easy Shredded Beef Tacos

Slow Cooked Pot Roast
Serves 4 with leftovers

Ingredients:

2 tablespoons vegetable oil
1 4-5 pound pot roast
1 packet taco seasoning (MS1)
1 onion, sliced
2 potatoes, peeled and cubed
3 cups beef stock (TS4)

Directions:

1. Heat a large Dutch oven over medium heat. Add the vegetable oil, followed by the roast. Sear the roast until browned on all sides.
2. Add the onions, potatoes, and stock.
3. Bring to a simmer, cover and cook over low heat for 3-4 hours, until the pot roast falls apart easily with a fork.

Easy Shredded Beef Tacos
Serves 4-6

Ingredients:

1. 1/2 leftover beef from pot roast
2. Taco shells (I buy a combination of crispy shells and soft tortillas; get whatever you like best)
3. Shredded lettuce
4. Shredded cheese
5. Salsa

Directions:

Heat the pot roast in the microwave, and warm the taco shells in a hot oven (350 degrees for about 10 minutes) and set up a taco bar with the remaining ingredients. Let everyone make their own tacos.

Tomato Braised Chicken Turns into Delicious Creamy Chicken Stew

Tomato Braised Chicken
Serves 3 with leftovers

Ingredients:

2 tablespoons vegetable oil
6 boneless, skinless chicken breasts
2 15-ounce cans diced tomatoes, with juices
1 tablespoon Italian seasoning
1 cup chicken stock (TS4)

Directions:

1. Heat the oil in a large skillet over medium heat. Add the chicken and sear until browned on both sides. Add the tomatoes, Italian seasoning, and chicken stock.
2. Simmer over low heat for 20-25 minutes, until chicken is cooked through.
3. Shred the chicken and serve over rice or pasta.

Delicious Creamy Chicken Stew
Serves 4

Ingredients:

1/2 recipe leftover shredded tomato braised chicken, including tomatoes and liquid
4 cups chicken stock (TS4)
2 cans evaporated milk
2 cups cooked rice

Directions:

1. Combine all ingredients in a large saucepot. Simmer over low heat until heated through.

Traditional Sloppy Joes Turns into Spicy Chili

Traditional Sloppy Joes
Serves 4-6 with leftovers

Ingredients:

2 pounds ground beef
1 cup chopped onion (TS3)
1/2 cup chopped green bell pepper
1 teaspoon garlic powder
1 cup ketchup
2 tablespoons brown sugar
2 teaspoons yellow mustard
Hamburger buns, for serving

Directions:

1. Heat a large skillet over medium heat. Add the ground beef, onions and bell peppers and cook until beef is no longer pink in the center. Add the garlic powder, ketchup, brown sugar and mustard and bring to a simmer. Simmer for 10 minutes, until heated through. Serve on hamburger buns.

Spicy Chili
Serves 4-6

Ingredients:

1/2 recipe leftover Traditional Sloppy Joes
2 cans diced tomatoes
2 tablespoons chili powder
1 cup chicken or beef stock (TS4)

Directions:

1. Combine all ingredients in a large sauce pot and bring to a simmer. Simmer for 15-20 minutes before serving.

Tip: I love to serve this chili with additional chopped onions, sour cream, and shredded cheddar and it is DELICIOUS! My family loves on a cold night when you just don't want to go anywhere or do anything!

Chicken and Tomato Stew Turns into Baked Pasta Casserole

Chicken and Tomato Stew
Serves 2 with leftovers

Ingredients:

2 tablespoons vegetable oil
1 cup chopped onion (TS3)
4 boneless skinless chicken breasts, cubed
1 packet Italian dressing seasoning (MS8)
3 cans diced tomatoes, plus juices
2 cups chicken stock (TS4)

Directions:

1. Heat the oil in a large stockpot. Add the chopped onion and cook until soft. Add the chicken and cook until browned on all sides, and then add the seasoning. Stir and add the tomatoes and broth.
2. Simmer for 20 minutes before serving.

Baked Pasta Casserole
Serves 4

Ingredients:

1/2 recipe Chicken and Tomato Stew, minus liquid
1/2 pound cooked penne pasta
1/2 cup shredded mozzarella cheese
1/2 cup grated Parmesan cheese

Directions:

1. Preheat oven to 400 degrees F.
2. Combine the chicken and tomato stew with the pasta in a 9x13 baking dish.
3. Cover and bake for 20 minutes.
4. Uncover, top with the cheeses and bake for 10 more minutes, until cheese is bubbly and lightly browned.

Stuffed Chicken Breasts with Broccoli Turns into Barbecue Chicken and Vegetable Pizza

Stuffed Chicken Breasts with Broccoli
Serves 4 with leftovers

Ingredients:

6 boneless skinless chicken breasts
1 box stuffing mix, prepared according to package directions
2 tablespoons vegetable oil
1 bag frozen broccoli florets

Directions:

1. Preheat oven to 350 degrees F. Spray a baking sheet with cooking spray.
2. Using a pairing knife, make a slit on the side of each chicken breast, being careful not to cut all the way through.
3. Stuff each breast with a couple tablespoons of the stuffing mix, and seal the edges with water. Lay on the baking sheet. Brush the tops with half the oil.
4. Toss the broccoli with the remaining oil and scatter around the chicken on the pan.
5. Bake for 30-35 minutes, until chicken is cooked through and broccoli is tender.

Barbecue Chicken and Vegetable Pizza
Serves 4

Ingredients:

1 large ready made pizza crust
1/2 cup barbecue sauce
2 servings leftover Stuffed Chicken Breasts with Broccoli
1 red onion, sliced
1/2 cup shredded cheddar cheese

Directions:

1. Preheat oven to 400 degrees F. Chop the chicken breasts, including the stuffing. Lay the pizza crust on a baking sheet. Spread with the barbecue sauce.

2. Top with the cooked broccoli and red onion, followed by cheese.
3. Bake for 10-12 minutes, until cheese is melted and crust is lightly browned.

Tip: For another variation, use Ranch dressing instead of Barbecue sauce for a delicious and easy white pizza!

Asian Pot Roast Turns into Stir Fry with Snow Peas and Mandarin Oranges

Asian Pot Roast
Serves 4-6 with leftovers

Ingredients:

2 tablespoons vegetable oil
1 4-5 pound pot roast
1 onion, sliced
1/4 cup soy sauce
1/4 cup Asian sesame salad dressing
2 1/2 cups beef stock (TS4)
Hot cooked rice, for serving

Directions:

1. Heat a large Dutch oven over medium heat. Add the vegetable oil, followed by the roast. Sear the roast until browned on all sides.
2. Add the onions, soy sauce, salad dressing, and stock.
3. Bring to a simmer, cover and cook over low heat for 3-4 hours, until the pot roast falls apart easily with a fork.

Stir Fry with Snow Peas and Mandarin Oranges

Serves 4-6

Ingredients:

1 tablespoon vegetable oil
2 cups snow pea pods
1 tablespoon soy sauce
1 cup mandarin oranges and juice
1/2 recipe leftover Asian pot roast, shredded
Hot cooked rice, for serving

Directions:

1. Heat the vegetable oil in a large skillet. Add the pea pods and cook, stirring, for 1 minute. Add the soy sauce, oranges, and juice. Stir and add the leftover beef.
2. Stir until heated through and serve over the rice.

Chicken and Roasted Vegetables Turns into White Chicken Lasagna

Chicken and Roasted Vegetables
Serves 3 with leftovers

Ingredients:

6 boneless skinless chicken breasts
2 bags frozen Italian vegetables
1 cup Italian salad dressing

Directions:

1. Preheat oven to 400 degrees F. Spray a large sheet pan with cooking spray.
2. Toss the chicken and veggies with the salad dressing. Spread on the sheet pan.
3. Bake until veggies are tender and chicken is cooked through, 35-40 minutes.

White Chicken Lasagna
Serves 4-6

Ingredients:

1/2 recipe Chicken and Roasted Vegetables
1 box lasagna noodles
1 32-ounce jar Alfredo sauce
1 cup shredded mozzarella cheese
1/2 cup grated Parmesan cheese

Directions:

1. Preheat oven to 350 degrees F. Spray a 9x13 casserole dish with cooking spray.
2. Chop the leftover chicken. Layer the chicken, lasagna noodles (you don't have to cook them!), Alfredo sauce, and cheeses, finishing with a layer of cheese.
3. Cover the pan tightly with foil and bake for 1 hour.
4. Remove from oven, uncover and allow to sit for 15 minutes before slicing.

Spicy Chicken Fajitas Turns into Fajita Omelets

Spicy Chicken Fajitas
Serves 6 with leftovers

Ingredients:

2 tablespoons vegetable oil
2 pounds chicken breast, cut into strips
2 packages fajita seasoning
2 packages frozen peppers and onions
1/2 cup water
Flour tortillas, warmed for serving

Directions:

1. Heat a large skillet over medium heat. Add the vegetable oil and chicken breasts. Cook until chicken is browned all over.
2. Add the fajita seasoning and peppers, followed by water. Simmer until vegetables are tender.
3. Serve the mixture in the warm tortillas.

Open Face Fajita Omelet
Serves 1

Ingredients: (per omelet)

3 eggs
1 tablespoon milk
1 teaspoon vegetable oil
1/2 cup leftover fajita vegetables, minus liquid
1/4 cup shredded cheddar cheese

Directions:

1. Beat the eggs with the milk. Heat a small nonstick skillet over medium heat. Add the oil and eggs and allow to cook until edges are set.
2. Add the vegetables. Cook for another minute and add the cheese. Continue cooking until eggs are cooked through.

Curried Chicken and Chickpeas Turns into Coconut Chicken Stew

Curried Chicken and Chickpeas
Serves 4-6 with leftovers

Ingredients:

2 tablespoons vegetable oil
1 cup chopped onion (TS3)
2 pounds chicken breasts, cubed
2 tablespoons curry powder
1 cup chicken stock (TS4)
2 cans chickpeas, drained
Hot cooked rice, for serving

Directions:

1. Heat a large skillet over medium heat and add the oil, followed by the onions. Cook until soft and add the chicken.
2. Cook until chicken is browned on all sides and add the curry powder, stock and chickpeas. Simmer for 10 minutes. Serve over the rice.

Coconut Chicken Stew
Serves 4-6

Ingredients:

1/2 recipe Curried Chicken and Chickpeas
3 cups chicken stock (TS4)
1 can coconut milk

Directions:

1. Combine the Curried chicken with the stock in a saucepan. Bring to a boil.
2. Reduce to a simmer and add the coconut milk. Stir and simmer until heated through.

Baked Chicken and Potatoes Turns into Chicken and Potato Quiche

Baked Chicken and Potatoes
Serves 4 with leftovers

Ingredients:

2 tablespoons vegetable oil
6 boneless skinless chicken breasts
1 packet ranch seasoning
3 large baking potatoes, peeled and diced

Directions:

1. Preheat oven to 400 degrees F. Spray a baking sheet with cooking spray.
2. Toss the chicken with the vegetable oil, ranch seasoning and cubed potatoes. Lay on sheet tray.
3. Bake for 30-35 minutes, until chicken is cooked through and potatoes are tender.

Tip: I like to serve this meal on a Friday or Saturday night if I'm having breakfast or brunch guests so that I can make the delicious quiche with little to no prep. The Ranch seasoning gives your quiche an herb-like flavor that tastes delicious with the classic egg dish.

Chicken and Potato Quiche
Serves 6-8

Ingredients:

1 pre-rolled piecrust
6 eggs
1 can condensed cream of mushroom soup
1/2 cup milk
1/2 recipe Baked Chicken and Potatoes
1/2 cup grated Parmesan cheese

Directions:

1. Preheat oven to 400 degrees F. Lay the pie crust in a pie plate and crimp the edges, cutting off excess. Chop the cooked chicken.
2. Beat the eggs with the mustard. Stir in the soup and milk. Add the chicken and potatoes and pour the mixture into the prepared pie crust. Sprinkle the cheese on top.
3. Bake for 25-30 minutes until eggs are set and cheese is browned.

Meals That Will Feed a Crowd

Whether you have a small family or a large one, sometimes you need a dinner that will feed a lot of people. Maybe it's for a big family party, or maybe you just want to have leftovers. Whatever the reason, you'll find what you're looking for in this section.

The best part is that even though you're making a lot of food, you still don't need to do a ton of prep work for a delicious crowd-pleasing meal. Need more than the recipe calls for? These recipes are also easy to double or even triple. This section is full of recipes that both adults and kids will love!

Slow Cooked Pulled Pork
Serves 12-16

Ingredients:

1 3-4 pound pork shoulder
2 cans root beer
2 16-ounce bottles barbecue sauce
Hamburger buns, for serving

Directions:

1. Preheat oven to 325 degrees F.
2. Put the pork and the root beer in a large Dutch oven. Cover and put it in the oven and cook for 4-6 hours, until pork shreds easily.
3. Drain the liquid, shred the pork and put back in the pot. Stir in the barbecue sauce, and serve.

Tip: This is the perfect type of recipe for a slow cooker if you have one. You can cook the meal in your cooker, and keep it warm for serving large groups.

No Fuss Lasagna
Serves 8-10

Ingredients:

1 pound ground beef
1 32-ounce jar marinara sauce
1 box lasagna noodles (you DON'T need to buy those no boil noodles; trust me!)
1 16-ounce container ricotta cheese
4 cups shredded mozzarella cheese

Directions:

1. Preheat oven to 350 degrees F. Spray a 9x13 casserole dish with cooking spray.
2. Heat the ground beef in a skillet and cook until no longer pink in the center. Stir in the marinara sauce.
3. Starting with the sauce, layer the sauce, noodles, ricotta, and mozzarella, ending with a layer of mozzarella. Spray a piece of foil with cooking spray and cover the dish.
4. Bake for 1 hour and remove the foil. Continue baking for 15 minutes, until cheese is melted. Allow to stand for 15 minutes before serving.

Tip: This is one of my favorite dishes for company for a few reasons: 1. Everyone loves it; who doesn't like lasagna? 2. It's easy to put together and get in the oven, and 3. You can put it together a day or two in advance, store it in the fridge and bake the day of. Just make sure that you let it sit out of the fridge for a half hour before you bake it, especially if your casserole dish is glass!

Easy Mac and Cheese
Serves 8-10

Ingredients:

1 pound macaroni noodles, cooked according to package directions
4 cups shredded cheddar cheese
1 cup milk
Salt and pepper

Directions:

1. Preheat oven to 375 degrees F.
2. Layer the cooked pasta and cheese in a large casserole dish, seasoning with salt and pepper as you go.
3. Pour the milk over top and bake for 1 hour until cheese is melted.

Sausage and Pepper Casserole
Serves 8-10

Ingredients:

1 pound penne pasta, cooked according to the package directions
1 tablespoon vegetable oil
1 pound Italian sausage links, sliced
1 bag frozen peppers and onions
1 32 ounce jar marinara sauce
1 cup mozzarella cheese

Directions:

1. Preheat oven to 350 degrees F. Spray a 9x13 casserole dish with cooking spray.
2. While your pasta is cooking, heat a skillet over medium heat and add the oil and the sausage. Cook until browned and add the peppers and marinara sauce. Simmer for 10 minutes and add the pasta. Transfer to casserole dish.
3. Bake for 30 minutes and remove from oven. Top with cheese and bake for 15 more minutes, or until cheese is melted.

Italian Fettuccine Pot
Serves 8-10

Ingredients:

6 cups chicken broth (TS4)
1 pound fettuccine noodles, broken in half
2 8-ounce packages frozen chopped spinach
2 28-ounce cans diced tomatoes with juices
1 cup chopped onion
1 teaspoon garlic powder
1 packet Italian dressing seasoning
1 pound Italian sausages, sliced and cooked
1 cup shredded mozzarella cheese

Directions:

1. Bring the stock to a rolling boil in a large pot. Add the pasta and and the tomatoes, spinach, onion, garlic powder, and seasoning. Cover and boil for 1 minute.
2. Reduce heat to medium, and continue cooking for 15 minutes, stirring every 3-4 minutes.
3. When the pasta is cooked, stir in the cooked sausage and cheese.

Cheesy Loaded Chicken and Potato Casserole

Serves 10

Ingredients:

1 16-ounce bag frozen hash brown potatoes, thawed
1 cup sour cream
1 packet Ranch dressing seasoning (MS6)
8 slices bacon, cooked and crumbled (TS6)
4 cups chopped or shredded cooked chicken (TS2)
3 cups shredded cheddar cheese
1/4 cup chopped green onions

Directions:

1. Preheat oven to 350 degrees F. Spray a 9x13 casserole dish with cooking spray.
2. Combine the potatoes, sour cream and ranch seasoning in a large bowl.
3. Layer the potato mixture, bacon, chicken and cheese in the casserole dish, ending with a layer of cheese.
4. Cover and bake for 30 minutes. Uncover and continue baking for 10 more minutes, until cheese is lightly browned and bubbly. Top with the green onions before serving.

Tip: This is my favorite side dish to go along with the Slow Cooked Pulled Pork in this section. Everyone loves it, and it's a perfect, comforting meal to feed a crowd!

Cheesy Spinach and Artichoke Pasta Pot
Serves 8-10

6 cups chicken broth (TS4)
1 pound fettuccine noodles, broken in half
1 8-ounce package frozen chopped spinach
1 8-ounce package frozen artichoke hearts
2 28-ounce cans diced tomatoes with juices
1 cup chopped onion
1 teaspoon garlic powder
1 packet Italian dressing seasoning
2 cups chopped or shredded cooked chicken (TS2)
1/2 cup grated Parmesan cheese
1 cup shredded mozzarella cheese

Directions:

1. Bring the stock to a rolling boil in a large pot. Add the pasta and and the tomatoes, spinach, artichokes, onion, garlic powder, and seasoning. Cover and boil for 1 minute.
2. Reduce heat to medium, and continue cooking for 15 minutes, stirring every 3-4 minutes.
3. When the pasta is cooked, stir in the cooked chicken and cheeses.

Cold Night Chili Con Carne
Serves 10-12

Ingredients:

2 pounds ground beef
1 cup chopped onion
1 packet chili seasoning mix (I only use Chili-O by French's)
2 cans kidney beans, undrained
2 cans diced tomatoes, undrained

Directions:

1. Cook the ground beef and onion in a large pot until beef is no longer pink in the center.
2. Add the rest of the ingredients and bring to a boil. Reduce heat to a simmer and simmer for 45-60 minutes before serving.

Tip: I love to serve this easy chili by putting out bowls of toppings everyone loves. Chopped onions, grated cheese, green onions, and some cornbread make this a fabulous winter meal that anyone will enjoy.

Cheesy Baked Ziti
Serves 8-10

Ingredients:

1 pound ziti pasta, cooked according to the package directions
1 pound 90 % lean ground beef
1 32-ounce jar marinara sauce
2 cups water
1/2 cup grated Parmesan
2 cups mozzarella cheese

Directions:

1. Preheat oven to 350 degrees F. Spray a 9x13 casserole dish with cooking spray.
2. While your pasta is cooking, heat a skillet over medium heat and add the ground beef. Cook until browned and add the marinara sauce and water. Simmer for 10 minutes and add the pasta and half of the cheese. Transfer to casserole dish.
3. Bake for 30 minutes and remove from oven. Top with remaining cheese and bake for 15 more minutes, or until cheese is melted.

Chicken and Dumpling Soup
Serves 10-12

Ingredients:

4 cups cooked and chopped chicken (breasts work fine, but I like both white and dark meat for this. I almost always cook a whole roasted chicken for this dish; see how in the Make Ahead section)
8 cups chicken stock (TS4)
1 can condensed cream of chicken soup
1 can condensed cream of mushroom soup
1 bag frozen mixed vegetables (peas, carrots, and corn)
2 large potatoes, peeled and cubed
2 cans refrigerated biscuits

Directions:

1. Combine all of the ingredients except the biscuits in a large pot or Dutch oven.
2. Bring to a boil, reduce heat and simmer for 1 hour.
3. About 20 minutes before serving, cut the biscuits into quarters. Drop them in the soup, and continue simmering 15-20 minutes.

Easiest Pasta Sauce EVER
Serves 10-12

Ingredients:

4 28-ounce cans whole peeled tomatoes
1/2 stick butter
1/2 onion, left whole
Cooked pasta, for serving

Directions:

1. Combine the tomatoes and butter in a large pot. Add the half onion and bring to a boil. Reduce heat to a simmer and cook for 45 minutes. Use tongs to break up the tomatoes.
2. If you like a chunky sauce, it's ready to serve. For a smooth, velvety sauce, puree in a blender. Serve over the pasta.

Tip: This is a perfect dish when you want something simple and home cooked but don't want to chop ingredients and simmer all day. I love to watch my guests faces when they first try this sauce, because it's just THAT delicious. You don't even need to add any seasoning to this sauce, just spoon it over your pasta. Trust me!

Extra Tip: This sauce is easy to prepare, and can be used in any of the recipes in this book that call for marinara sauce. Make up a big batch and eat it with pasta, in lasagna, or wherever you want; the possibilities are endless!

Chicken Salsa Verde Enchilada Casserole
Serves 8-10

Ingredients:

4 cups chopped or shredded cooked chicken (TS2)
2 16-ounce jars Salsa Verde
2 cups shredded cheese
16 corn tortillas

Ingredients:

1. Preheat oven to 350 degrees F. Spray a 9x13 casserole dish with cooking spray.
2. Combine the chicken, salsa and half the cheese in a large bowl.
3. Layer the chicken mixture with the tortillas in the casserole dish.
4. Cover and bake for 30 minutes. Uncover and top with remaining cheese. Bake for 10 more minutes until cheese is melted.
5. Allow to stand for 10 minutes before slicing and serving.

Lasagna Soup
Serves 8-10

Ingredients:

1 tablespoon vegetable oil
1 cup chopped onion
1 pound Italian sausages, removed from casings
1 packet Italian dressing seasoning
2 15-ounce cans crushed tomatoes
6 cups chicken stock (TS4)
1 box lasagna noodles, broken into pieces
1 5-ounce can evaporated milk
Grated Parmesan cheese, for serving

Directions:

1. Heat a large pot over medium heat. Add the onions and sausages and cook until sausages is browed. Add the seasoning and stir.
2. Add the tomatoes and stock and bring to a boil. Add the lasagna noodles and simmer for 15 minutes, or until noodles are tender.
3. Stir in the evaporated milk, heat through and stir.
4. Top hot bowls with the cheese before serving.

Four Cheese Baked Penne
Serves 8-10

Ingredients:

1 pound penne pasta, cooked according to the package directions
2 32-ounce jars marinara sauce
1/2 cup grated Parmesan
1 cup shredded mozzarella cheese
1 cup shredded cheddar cheese
10 slices Provolone cheese

Directions:

1. Preheat oven to 350 degrees F. Spray a 9x13 casserole dish with cooking spray.
2. Combine the pasta, sauce, Parmesan, mozzarella, and cheddar cheese in the casserole dish.
3. Lay the slices of Provolone on top. Bake for 20 minutes, until cheese is melted and bubbly.

Index

Chickpeas

Chili

Corn

Tortellini

Tortillas

Turkey